THE
HUMMUS
COOKBOOK

THE
HUMMUS
COOKBOOK

Deliciously different ways with the versatile classic

SARA LEWIS

photography by William Shaw

LORENZ BOOKS

This edition is published by Lorenz Books
an imprint of Anness Publishing Ltd
info@anness.com

www.lorenzbooks.com; www.annesspublishing.com

© Anness Publishing Ltd 2020

Publisher: Joanna Lorenz
Photography: William Shaw
Food for photography: Sara Lewis
Designer: Adelle Mahoney
Styling: Pene Parker
Editorial: Sarah Lumby

ACKNOWLEDGEMENTS
A big thank you to Magimix for the loan of the food
processors used in the step-by-step pictures in this book.

COOK'S NOTES
Bracketed terms are intended for American readers.
For all recipes, quantities are given in both metric and
imperial measures and, where appropriate, in standard cups
and spoons. Follow one set of measures, but not a mixture,
because they are not interchangeable.
Standard spoon and cup measures are level.
1 tsp = 5ml, 1 tbsp = 15ml, 1 cup = 250ml/8fl oz.
Australian standard tablespoons are 20ml. Australian
readers should use 3 tsp in place of 1 tbsp for measuring
small quantities. American pints are 16fl oz/2 cups.
American readers should use 20fl oz/2.5 cups in place of 1
pint when measuring liquids.
Electric oven temperatures in this book are for conventional
ovens. When using a fan oven, the temperature will
probably need to be reduced by about 10–20°C/20–40°F.
Since ovens vary, you should check with your manufacturer's
instruction book for guidance.
The nutritional analysis given for each recipe is calculated
per portion (i.e. serving or item), unless otherwise stated. If
the recipe gives a range, such as Serves 4–6, then the
nutritional analysis will be for the smaller portion size, i.e. 6
servings. The analysis does not include optional ingredients,
such as salt added to taste.

Contents

Introduction

Hummus, hoummus, hommos or humus is a chickpea dip made for hundreds of years in the Middle East as a staple peasant food. Known as hummus bi tahini in Arabic it quite literally translates to chickpeas with tahini, the two main ingredients that go into hummus. Chickpeas, sometimes known as garbanzo beans, are mixed with tahini, which is a sesame seed paste, and fresh lemon juice until it forms a soft ultra-smooth spoonable dip.

First written about in Britain in the 1950s by the great food writer Elizabeth David, it wasn't until the 1980s that hummus began to be sold in a mainstream supermarket. Its popularity grew as more and more families began to travel and enjoy European holidays – developing from a fringe, slightly 'hippy' dip to something that can now be found in most people's refrigerators. It is thought that Britain alone consumes 12,000 tonnes a year, with even more sold in the USA.

Traditionally served with just a drizzle of olive oil and a little paprika, hummus is now available customised with all kinds of toppings – red onion, fresh green herbs or piri piri – and even mixed with other vegetables such as roasted red bell pepper, broad or fava beans, or avocado. In the USA you can even buy peanut butter and chocolate flavours. From its ancient beginnings, hummus has been adapted by each country that has discovered it, and made it their own.

Hummus not only tastes good but is also seen as healthy: although not a low-calorie food, it contains 'smart carbs' or carbohydrates that are slow to digest, so leaving you feeling fuller for longer, while also being a good source of protein and low in fat.

In the Middle East most families make their own hummus, and you too can make hummus easily at home – creamy smooth and even better than shop-bought. You'll know exactly what it contains, salt levels can be reduced, and there are no hidden preservatives to extend the shelf life.

Right: Hummus isn't just an appetizer or dip, it is also wonderful used as a base for spiced meat or vegetables in a main meal.

Usually made with dried chickpeas which need soaking in cold water overnight then boiled until soft, canned chickpeas offer a speedier and easily accessible alternative if you prefer. Blend the cooked chickpeas in a food processor or with a stick blender then flavour with garlic, cumin or your own favourite additions. You can tinker around with the basic recipe, adding more lemon juice, less tahini, perhaps some extra olive oil, melted butter or even some yogurt for a lighter taste. Begin with the amounts suggested in the recipes and then when you have worked out which elements you like the best, gradually increase. Just remember once the ingredient is added, there is no taking it out, so add little by little and keep tasting.

Hummus is so much more than just a dip. Serve it spooned over plates as a base for meatballs, barbecued skewers or slow-cooked tagines or casseroles in much the same way that you would serve rice or mashed potatoes. Spread hummus over bread instead of butter, in place of cream cheese over bagels, or mix with a little extra olive oil or water and substitute for mayonnaise or creamy salad dressings. Try spreading it over the base of a puff pastry tart then top with roasted vegetables, or wrap in filo pastry for a borek in place of the more traditional cream cheese. You can add it as a layer in sandwiches and tortilla wraps, bake it on fish, and you can even add hummus to muffins. No wonder the long-loved hummus is also the health food of the future!

Left: Hummus is traditionally flavoured with garlic, salt and cayenne pepper, as well as olive oil and lemon juice.

History of hummus

Claimed by many as their own – whether Israeli, Egyptian, Syrian, Lebanese, Greek or Turkish – it seems everyone has been eating hummus in the Middle East and Eastern Mediterranean for hundreds if not thousands of years. In these regions, parts of which were once known as the Levant, hummus is typically served as part of a mezze or range of little dishes. As well as the hummus drizzled with olive oil these dishes can include falafel, the aubergine or eggplant dip baba ganoush, the yogurt-based cacik, and tabbouleh salad, along with many other popular items. Hummus is also served with the main course, perhaps spread over a plate and topped with slow-cooked meats or barbecued skewers of meat or fish.

There is an early mention of hummus in Cairo, Egypt, during the 13th century, where it appears with vinegar – but

Below: Hummus can be seasoned as you like but a sprinkling of cayenne and black pepper is popular, with olive oil as an accompaniment.

no lemon or garlic – in a recipe entitled 'hummus kasa'. A Syrian cookbook of the same period has a recipe with puréed chickpeas and lemons. However, it wasn't until the 18th century in Damascus that a recipe for hummus bi tahini is mentioned, which combines tahini with the chickpeas.

The exact origins may be lost in time but the essential ingredients of hummus have been cultivated in the Middle East for thousands of years. Chickpeas have even been discovered in archaeological digs before pottery was invented, so were being eaten some 10,000 years ago. We know sesame oil has been made in Mesopotamia since 2500BCE, and garlic was recorded in the ancient pyramids of Giza. These staples were grown and spread further afield as the trade routes expanded, as did the dishes made with them. Each country adapted and made hummus in their own style, although all commonly agree that it must be made with chickpeas, tahini and lemon juice. Some then add garlic, some cumin. Most countries serve hummus drizzled with olive oil. Turkey serves it with melted butter or buttery fried garlic – others add yogurt for a lighter-textured hummus. In Israel, hummus is so popular there are special hummusia, small cafés that specialize only in hummus, and the question of which café creates the best version is a subject of hot debate and discussion. Much loved by all, the better question is not where it originated but how to make and enjoy the best version you can!

Above left: Hummus is traditionally served as part of a mezze, a spread of little savoury dishes.
Above middle: Hummus is so popular in Israel that there are cafés specialising in it!
Above right: Add a little extra lemon juice and water, and hummus makes a great dressing.

Packed with good health

Above and opposite: Hummus fits perfectly into a healthier lifestyle and cleaner way of cooking. Chickpeas make a great and cheap store–cupboard standby and can be easily transformed into a versatile dish that is so much more than a dip.

Hummus is wonderful to eat but is also packed full with nutrients. It is an excellent source of protein, especially for those who do not eat meat. Protein forms part of the essential building blocks for bone, muscle, skin and blood health. Plus, it helps us to feel full and satiated – a serving of hummus will make you feel satisfied rather than hungry.

Dried legumes, a family group of which chickpeas are part, contain three compounds, saponins, protease inhibitors and phytic acid, which are thought to help protect cells from damage that can lead to cancer.

Chickpeas are rich in fibre which not only keeps our digestive tract in good working order but helps to promote the growth of beneficial bacteria in the digestive system, especially in the colon. Fibre is also part of the food group of carbohydrates. These complex carbs, often known as good carbs, are digested slowly so can help to fight hunger cravings and to balance sugar levels, which helps to avoid mood swings. The fibre in chickpeas may also help to lower LDL cholesterol.

Chickpeas are low in fat, and although hummus has small amounts of fat in the tahini and olive oil, these are mainly monounsaturated fats. Both chickpeas and tahini contain calcium which contributes to good bone health. Calcium is needed by children for growing skeletons but is just as important for seniors to maintain bone strength and help to prevent osteoporosis.

Chickpeas and tahini also contain small amounts of iron which is needed by the body to help keep red blood cells oxygenated. There are trace amounts of other vitamins and minerals too – folates, vitamin A, thiamine, riboflavin, niacin and vitamin B-6.

It is important to watch the amount of salt or sodium that you consume. Making your own hummus means that you know exactly how much salt there is. Salt levels can be reduced further by adding stronger flavourings such as herbs, roasted vegetables, spices and garlic.

The Mediterranean diet: Hummus features in the Mediterranean diet which has long been considered as super-healthy. Rich in vegetables, dried legumes, fruit, nuts and olive oil with smaller amounts of fish and meat, it is thought that a high percentage of heart disease could be prevented by switching to a Mediterranean diet.

Gluten-free: All the ingredients in homemade hummus are also gluten-free, although unfortunately the breads usually served with it are not. Choose instead from a wide range of veggy dippers and buy specialist gluten-free breads or have a go at making your own. On page 141 there is an easy gluten-free gram or chickpea flour and rice flour flatbread.

Dairy-free: Hummus is suitable for dairy-free diets providing that you do not add butter or yogurt, although dairy-free yogurts may be substituted. Where butter is used to drizzle over hummus just substitute with a spoonful or two of olive oil.

Vegetarian and vegan: Hummus fits perfectly into a vegetarian or stricter vegan diet where meat and fish is off the menu. For those following a vegan diet, butter and yogurt is not permitted, but olive oil makes a tastier and equally luxurious alternative.

Nut-free: None of the recipes in this book are made with peanuts although a couple of recipes do contain a mix of other nuts. Please read the recipes carefully to double check that they are suitable.

Paleo: Often called the caveman diet, this low-carb diet goes back to hunter-gatherer basics and so homemade hummus fits perfectly, freshly made at home with no additives or preservatives and served with a mix of vegetables or meaty toppings. Refined white flours and sugars are off the menu, along with man-made fats such as butter and margarine.

Left: Topped with herbs, served with roasted pepper, spread on to wraps: the chickpea dip is incredibly versatile.

All about chickpeas

Above: Always check over dried chickpeas before soaking them in water, and discard any that are discoloured.

Hummus is traditionally made with dried chickpeas, sometimes called garbanzo beans, which are preservative-free, cheap and readily available in supermarkets and health food stores, and make a great store-cupboard standby. There are two camps, with the purists who say that you can only make hummus with dried chickpeas and the more modern cooks who say canned are the way to go for speed and convenience. Both work very well!

SOAKING IS KEY
Dried chickpeas must be soaked in cold water before cooking. It takes just a few minutes to add the dried chickpeas to a bowl, cover with plenty of cold water then leave overnight or for at least 8 hours. Some recipes give definitive amounts of water to chickpeas, but this is not essential – aim for about three times the amount of water to dried chickpeas so that they are generously covered with water. Cover the top of the bowl with a plate, clear film or plastic wrap and leave in a cool place, or refrigerator if you have room.

HOW TO COOK CHICKPEAS
Next day, drain the now swollen and plumped-up chickpeas into a colander then tip into a large pan, cover with cold water and bring to the boil. Skim off any scum that forms with a spoon then simmer until tender. This can take anything up to 2 hours; you are aiming for the chickpeas to be so soft that you can press them between your finger and thumb.

The cooking process can be speeded up with the time-honoured trick of adding bicarbonate of soda (baking soda) to the cooking water. This prevents the calcium in hard city tap water from sticking to the pectin in the chickpea's cell walls. Adding bicarbonate of soda changes the water's pH to alkaline and this encourages the pectins to separate and the chickpeas to soften. Just 1.5ml/¼ tsp to 1 litre/1¾ pint/4 cups of water is all that is needed to soften 100g/3¾oz/½ cup dried weight of chickpeas.

Many cooks suggest adding more bicarbonate of soda and some even suggest adding bicarb to the soaking water too. Just be wary that adding too much bicarb will give the cooked chickpeas a soapy taste. It's all a matter of balance, to add just enough bicarb to help speed along the cooking but not at the expense of the finished flavour.

Even with the addition of bicarb the cooking time of the chickpeas will still vary depending on their size and age. The older the chickpeas are the longer they can take to cook. As with other dried pulses, don't add salt until the end of cooking as this can toughen the chickpeas.

Some recipes even say to peel the cooked chickpeas. Most of us wouldn't even realise that chickpeas have skins and the idea of peeling them seems a pretty fiddly business. During the long cooking required for making hummus some of the skins naturally separate from a few of the chickpeas, but there would still be many chickpeas left to skin. While skinned chickpeas do blend to a smoother-finished hummus, unless you are planning to enter a hummus competition or are doing a taste comparison, it really is not worth the time or effort and chances are your dinner guests would be none the wiser either way. Also, if you get side-tracked and the chickpeas cook for a little longer than you meant them to, it doesn't matter if some have broken up as they are going to be blended smooth anyway.

Above: Always soak dried chickpeas before use in plenty of cold water, ideally overnight or for a minimum of 8 hours.

BLENDING HUMMUS

Modern cooks wouldn't dream of making hummus without a food processor. Add the metal blade then simply add the drained cooked chickpeas and flavourings in the specified amounts and blend for 2–3 minutes until smooth. Taste and adjust the tahini, lemon juice or garlic. If your hummus looks a little coarse, gradually add extra water and blend again until really smooth with a creamy, softly spoonable texture.

If your food processor isn't quite tough enough or you only have a stick blender, then you may prefer to blend the tahini, lemon juice and a little cooking water or fresh water first to loosen the tahini. Add the cooked chickpeas and blend until smooth, adjusting with a little extra water if needed.

QUICK QUANTITY GUIDE		
Dried chickpeas =	Cooked chickpeas =	Hummus
100g/3¾oz	200–225g/7–8oz	275g/10oz
200g/7oz	400–450g/14oz–1lb	525g/1lb 2oz
300g/11oz	600–675g/1lb 6oz–1½lb	800g/1¾lb

GETTING THE RIGHT TEXTURE

Once the cooked chickpeas are flavoured with tahini and lemon juice they will require a little extra liquid to blend to a creamy smooth texture. Some cooks argue strongly that you must use a little of the water that the chickpeas were cooked in, others that the only liquid should be iced water. If you added bicarbonate of soda (baking soda) to the cooking water this can add a distinct flavour, especially in more generous amounts, and so this water is best not added to the finished hummus. Cooking water without bicarbonate of soda or just a tiny amount is fine. Much comes down to personal taste, as both options work well.

For fans of olive oil you may also like to blend in a tablespoon or two of olive oil as well as a drizzle over the top to finish. Or for a lighter texture a little Greek yogurt can be blended into the hummus, with a little less water.

Below: If you can soak and cook a large quantity of chickpeas and freeze in single-batch bags, it is easy to take out and defrost as needed.

Opposite, top to bottom: Other pulses can be soaked and blended in the same way to make interesting variations of hummus – you could try cannellini beans, borlotti beans or black beans.

CAN I USE A PRESSURE COOKER?
Yes, but it is important to refer to your pressure cooker handbook for full details on amounts of chickpeas, water and timings. Soak measured dried chickpeas in plenty of cold water overnight then drain and add to the pressure cooker with fresh water as specified in your handbook. Add the lid and bring up to pressure, lower the heat but maintain pressure, and time for 15 minutes or again as the handbook directs. Release the pressure by allowing the pressure cooker to cool for about 10 minutes for natural release, drain the chickpeas into a colander (reserving the cooking water if liked) and allow the chickpeas to cool before blending.

CAN YOU FREEZE COOKED CHICKPEAS?
As dried soaked chickpeas take a while to cook it makes sense to soak and cook a larger batch than you need. Double or even triple up the amount of chickpeas that you need from 100g/3¾oz/½ cup to 200g/7oz/generous 1 cup dried chickpeas or 300g/11oz/1½ cups of dried chickpeas. The soaking and cooking time stays the same so it makes sense.

Once cooked and drained divide in half or quarter, or if you forget how many chickpeas you started with, 200–225g/7–8oz/ 1 cup of cooked chickpeas = 100g/3¾oz/½ cup dried chickpeas. Pack chickpeas into plastic bags, press out the air, seal and label. You can freeze cooked chickpeas for up to 6 weeks. Defrost at room temperature for 3–4 hours depending on the size of bag. It is not advisable to freeze finished made hummus.

HELP I FORGOT TO SOAK THE CHICKPEAS!

While it is advisable to soak dried chickpeas in water overnight it is possible to reduce the soaking time for those emergency moments when you just plain forgot.

Add the dried chickpeas to a pan and generously cover with water, bring up to the boil and boil rapidly for 1 minute. Take the pan off the heat, cover with a lid and leave to cool for 1 hour. Drain off the water, add fresh measured water and bicarbonate of soda (baking soda), bring up to the boil, skim off any scum and simmer until tender as instructed in your chosen recipe. If time is just too tight then open a can, even two!

WHAT ABOUT CANNED CHICKPEAS?

Canned chickpeas in water and salt make a convenient and speedy alternative to home-cooked dried chickpeas. With no need for soaking and cooking, canned chickpeas can be flavoured and blended and the hummus ready to eat in just 10 minutes for a super-speedy, super-healthy snack lunch. One 400g/14oz can gives 240g/8¾oz drained weight of chickpeas.

WHAT ABOUT OTHER PULSES?

While we tend to think that hummus can only be made with chickpeas, dried split peas, cannellini beans or black beans can also be used. Soak overnight in plenty of cold water just like the chickpeas and then boil in water without bicarbonate of soda for about 1 hour until tender. Or try mung beans; these little green beans need soaking overnight but then cook in just 30 minutes.

If using dried red kidney beans, make sure to boil the beans rapidly for 10 minutes to destroy harmful levels of toxins then simmer until tender. These are the only dried beans that require the rapid boiling first.

How to make tahini

Traditionally you can't make hummus without tahini. This fine sesame seed paste is sold in jars in all Mediterranean food stores or health food stores and comes in a light or darker version. The light version is made with hulled sesame seeds, which have a whiter appearance and milder flavour.

Sesame seeds are healthy – they have more protein than milk and most nuts, as well as B vitamins to boost energy and brain function, and vitamin E to help protect against heart disease and stroke, along with the essential minerals magnesium, iron and calcium.

If you have a food processor or liquidiser, tahini is quick and easy to make at home with sesame seeds and a little olive oil. Stored in glass jars, it will settle with time, with the oil rising to the top leaving the thick sesame paste on the bottom, so make sure to stir before using.

Tahini also tastes great added to stir-fries, and mixed into smoothies or smoothie bowls instead of a spoonful of nut butter. Fork together tahini with lemon juice, a little water and some finely chopped garlic to create an easy salad dressing, or spread it over toast and drizzle with honey, date syrup or pomegranate molasses for a favourite Eastern Mediterranean snack. Tahini also forms the base of halva – a light crumbly sweet a little like nougat, which is delicious crumbled and mixed with whipped cream and yogurt for a cheat's ice cream or more exotic version of Eton mess.

Makes 125g/4¼oz/¾ cup

1 Choose hulled lighter-coloured sesame seeds, or for a stronger, darker-coloured tahini use mixed coloured seeds. Measure 100g/3¾oz of sesame seeds.

2 Tip the seeds into a dry frying pan and toast over a medium-low heat until golden brown, shaking the pan from time to time. Don't have

the heat too high or the seeds will pop out of the pan in much the same way as when making popcorn. Leave to cool for 10 minutes.

3 Tip the toasted sesame seeds into the bowl of a food processor or liquidiser goblet, add the lid then grind the seeds to a coarse powder.

4 Slowly drizzle 90ml/6 tbsp of olive oil through the lid and blend until a smooth paste.

5 Continue blending until smooth, scraping down the sides of the processor or liquidiser with a plastic spatula from time to time.

6 Spoon the tahini into a jar and screw on the lid. Keep in the refrigerator for up to 1 week.

Energy 664kcal/2779kJ; Protein 23.4g; Carbohydrate 0g, of which sugars 0g; Fat 62.5g, of which saturates 7.8g; Cholesterol 0mg; Calcium 0mg; Fibre 0g; Sodium 0mg.

Lemon, oil, seasoning

Making your own hummus is very much mix and taste, to get the right combinations of flavour to suit your palate. Add little by little as you can't reduce the amount once it is in.

LEMON

Add freshly squeezed lemon juice for a fresh-tasting zing to your hummus. Bottled lemon juice just doesn't give the same intensity of flavour. Keep the lemons at room temperature so that you can extract the maximum amount of juice. Add just the juice of half a lemon, making sure to discard any seeds first. Taste and then add a little extra lemon juice if needed.

OLIVE OIL

Many people assume that hummus has lots of olive oil in it, but traditionalists prefer to drizzle olive oil over the finished hummus rather than to add extra when mixing. Buy the best olive oil you can, as cheap vegetable or sunflower oil just won't give the same flavour. Much like wine, the flavour of olive oil varies depending on the region it came from. Choose extra virgin cold-pressed olive oil if possible. Cold-pressed oils mean that the oil is as natural as possible and contains higher amounts of monounsaturated fatty acids, polyphenols and antioxidants for added health benefits.

SEASONINGS

Just like lemon juice, add just a little salt and cayenne pepper at the beginning then taste and adjust the seasoning once the hummus has been mixed. Traditionally a little ground cumin, cayenne pepper or paprika is added, to boost the flavour.

GARLIC OR NOT?

Opinion is split on this, some purists prefer not to add garlic, but let diners stir in a little garlic sauce to taste at the table, while other cooks feel garlic is essential and should be added when blending the hummus. Again it is very much a personal choice.

How to make hummus

Making your own hummus really isn't difficult or time-consuming, the only thing is to remember to soak the dried chickpeas in cold water overnight. Drain next day, add to a pan with plenty of water, and leave to simmer. While it can take a while to cook the chickpeas, you don't need to stand over them – while they cook you can catch up with jobs around the house then simply blitz to a smooth purée in a food processor with flavourings, and that's it! This is the basic method, use the quantities specified in your chosen recipe (see page 36 for the classic hummus recipe).

1 Add 100g/3¾oz/½ cup dried chickpeas to a large bowl, pour over cold water to generously cover the dried chickpeas then cover and leave in a cool place overnight.

2 Drain the chickpeas into a colander then tip into a large pan. Pour over 1 litre/1¾ pint/4 cups water then stir in 1.5ml/¼ tsp bicarbonate of soda (baking soda).

3 Bring the water to the boil then skim off any scum that forms with a spoon. Half cover with a lid and leave the chickpeas to simmer over a medium heat for 45–75 minutes.

4 Test to see if the chickpeas are tender by scooping out a few from the pan with a spoon, leave to cool for a minute or two then see if they break easily when pressed between a finger and thumb. If they do, then tip the cooked chickpeas into a colander set over a bowl. Reserve the water if you plan to use it in your hummus rather than fresh water (see further information for this on pages 16–17). Cover the chickpeas with a clean dish towel and leave to cool for 30 minutes.

STORAGE TIP Once the hummus is made, spoon into a plastic container, spread the hummus level and cover with a lid. Store in the refrigerator for up to 3 days.

5 Add the cooked drained chickpeas to the bowl of a food processor fitted with a metal blade. Add 30ml/2 tbsp tahini, then squeeze in the juice of ½ lemon, discarding any pips. Season with salt and cayenne pepper.

6 Add 4–6 tbsp chickpea cooking water or fresh cold water if preferred. Add the lid to the food processor then blend for 2–3 minutes until smooth.

7 Taste the hummus and adjust the seasoning with extra salt and pepper, more tahini, lemon juice or extra cooking or fresh water, to make the flavour and consistency just how you like it. Blitz again until very smooth and the hummus is soft and creamy. Serve immediately or store covered in the refrigerator.

Perfect partners

Makes 150g/5oz/¾ cup
1 red (bell) pepper, quartered, cored and deseeded
5ml/1 tsp coriander seeds
2.5ml/½ tsp cumin seeds
1.5ml/¼ tsp caraway seeds
30ml/2 tbsp olive oil
1 red onion, chopped
3 garlic cloves, sliced
3 large red chillies, deseeded and chopped
10ml/2 tsp tomato purée (paste)
30ml/2 tbsp lemon juice
2.5ml/½ tsp salt

HARISSA

This mellow fiery condiment is made with roasted red pepper, red onion, hot red chillies and garlic then flavoured with roasted coriander, cumin and caraway seeds and mixed to a coarse paste with olive oil and tomato purée. You can make your own blend or buy readymade in small jars in most supermarkets. A version of this is sold as the sauce known as Sriracha.

Mix harissa with a little extra oil and drizzle over the top of hummus, mix with extra lemon juice to make an easy and tasty dressing for salad or couscous, or to add to meaty marinades. Serve tiny spoonfuls with roasted vegetables or mixed vegetable tagines or stews.

1 Put the red pepper on to a piece of foil skin-side up and grill or broil for 10 minutes until the skin is blackened and the peppers softened. Wrap in foil and leave to cool. Peel the skin from the peppers and add the flesh to a liquidiser goblet.

2 Crush the seeds in a pestle and mortar. Heat 15ml/1 tbsp oil in a frying pan, add the seeds and cook for 1 minute to release the flavour. Add the onion and fry for 5 minutes over a medium heat until softened. Add the garlic and chillies and fry for 5 minutes until softened and the onions are golden.

3 Stir in the tomato purée, lemon juice and salt then spoon into the liquidiser with the remaining oil. Add the lid and blend until smooth. Taste and adjust the salt if needed.

Energy 287kcal/1186kJ; Protein 3.4g; Carbohydrate 18g, of which sugars 15.8g; Fat 22.8g, of which saturates 3.3g; Cholesterol 0mg; Calcium 38mg; Fibre 5g; Sodium 1018mg.

ZA'ATAR SPICE MIX

This popular Middle Eastern spice mix is named after a wild herb that grows in abundance on the Syrian Lebanese mountains. For anyone who has grown up in this region, the smell of this herb just makes them think of home. Known as hyssop or Syrian oregano, it tastes a little like a cross between oregano and thyme. When in season the fresh leaves are added to tomato salad and breads or picked and hung in bunches to dry.

For za'atar, dried leaves are ground and mixed with lemony tasting sumac seeds, fragrant cumin and sesame seeds, and left with the texture of roughly crushed sesame seeds or finely ground to a green powder. Rather than using the herb za'atar, this recipe uses a mix of dried oregano and fresh thyme to recreate the flavour. Za'atar spice mix tastes delicious added to warmed butter then drizzled over hummus or mixed with oil and added to dressings, or sprinkled over labneh, a simple-to-make soft cheese.

1 Lightly toast the sesame seeds in a dry frying pan until just beginning to brown. Take off the heat and set aside.

2 Add the cumin seeds and sumac seeds to a pestle and mortar and roughly crush to release their flavour. Add the sesame seeds, the dried oregano, fresh thyme leaves and salt. Lightly crush together then spoon into a small jar. Screw on the lid and keep in the refrigerator for up to 2 weeks.

Makes 20g/¾oz/¼ cup
15ml/1 tbsp sesame seeds
5ml/1 tsp cumin seeds
5ml/1 tsp sumac seeds
5ml/1 tsp dried oregano
Small bunch fresh thyme, tear the leaves from the stems to give 15ml/1 tbsp
2.5ml/½ tsp salt flakes

PAPRIKA

This vibrant red spice is made from ground chillies and comes in two strengths: sweet or mild, and a much hotter, fiery version which is as hot as chilli powder. Look out for smoked paprika too, which again comes in the same two strengths; it is sometimes called pimenton on the container, and it adds a great barbecue-smoky flavour.

CHERMOULA SAUCE

This raw fresh herb and chilli sauce adds a vibrant green hue to any recipe. Serve as a topping to hummus, use as the base to a marinade, or simply spoon over barbecued foods.

Makes 100g/3¾oz/½ cup

2 garlic cloves, sliced

15g/½oz/1 handful of fresh flat leaf parsley

15g/½oz/1 handful of fresh coriander (cilantro)

1 large red or green chilli, halved, deseeded and sliced

5ml/1 tsp cumin seeds, roughly crushed in a pestle and mortar

30ml/2 tbsp olive oil

Juice of 1 lemon

Salt and cayenne pepper

1 Add the garlic, herbs and chilli to the bowl of a food processor or liquidiser. Add the cumin seeds, oil and lemon juice then add a little salt and pepper. Screw on the lid and blend until the herbs are very finely chopped, scraping down the sides of the goblet with a spatula as needed.

2 Spoon the herb sauce into a small jar and press the herbs beneath the level of the oil. Screw on the lid and chill in the refrigerator, and use within 24 hours.

Energy 221kcal/910kJ; Protein 1.8g; Carbohydrate 2.9g, of which sugars 2.8g; Fat 22.5g, of which saturates 3.1g; Cholesterol 0mg; Calcium 68mg; Fibre 2g; Sodium 16mg.

TARATOR SAUCE

Like chermoula sauce this fresh garlic herb sauce adds colour and zing, but rather than chilli it is flavoured with toasted walnuts and sesame seed tahini. Try it spooned or swirled into hummus or to accompany grilled or barbecued mackerel or hake, lamb skewers or roasted chicken and salad.

1 Dry-fry the walnut pieces in a nonstick frying pan for 3–4 minutes until lightly toasted then leave to cool for 10 minutes.

2 Add the walnuts to the bowl of a food processor with the garlic, parsley, tahini, lemon juice and oil. Season with a little salt and cayenne pepper then add the lid and blend until the nuts and herbs are very finely chopped.

3 Spoon into a small jar and press down so that the nuts and herbs are beneath the oil. Screw on the lid and chill in the refrigerator, and use within 24 hours.

**Makes 110g/4oz/
generous ½ cup**
50g/2oz/½ cup walnut pieces
1 garlic clove, sliced
20g/¾oz/large handful fresh
flat leaf parsley
10ml/2 tsp tahini
Juice of ½ lemon
30ml/2 tbsp olive oil
Salt and cayenne pepper

SUMAC

These tiny deep red or almost purple berries are dried and ground and can be sprinkled over hummus. They add a tangy, slightly sour flavour and can be used in place of lemon.

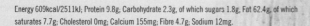

Energy 609kcal/2511kJ; Protein 9.8g; Carbohydrate 2.3g, of which sugars 1.8g, Fat 62.4g, of which saturates 7.7g; Cholesterol 0mg; Calcium 155mg; Fibre 4.7g; Sodium 12mg.

Dippers and dunkers

Hummus is a great healthy, high-protein low fat snack. Serve with warm pitta breads or flatbreads, or why not try making your own as shown on pages 130–143.

As well as bread you can of course serve homemade hummus with a wonderful range of crisp and crunchy vegetables. Choose from strips of brightly coloured red, yellow or orange (bell) pepper, carrot, celery or cucumber sticks. Try peppery-tasting

radishes or cool creamy cauliflower florets, or
the more unusual green-tinged space-age
romesco caulilflower, trimmed from the core and
cut into small bite-sized florets. You could spoon
hummus into baby lettuce, chicory and bitter endive
leaves. Cherry tomatoes are nice dipped into hummus, or
you could dollop it into scooped-out larger tomatoes. For
onion fans, cut a whole mild-tasting onion into 6 or 8 wedges
depending on its size, then separate the layers and use these
as scoops to dunk into the hummus. You could try the same
with aniseed-tasting fennel.

Some vegetables are just the right shape
for dunking and eating whole – fresh and
crisp mangetout or sugar snap peas, little
baby corn, a baby carrot or turnip, even
a tiny courgette or zucchini. These can
be eaten raw but you might prefer
others lightly boiled, still keeping
their al dente crispness – perhaps
asparagus stems, or green beans.
The best thing is to choose and
serve whatever looks freshest
on the day.

TRADITIONAL HUMMUS

The recipes in this chapter use dried chickpeas for the classic taste and texture. Soak in water the night before you need them, then cook next day until really soft and tender for a slightly nuttier authentic-tasting hummus. Serve simply with oil and paprika, chopped herbs, or buttery fried garlic, or yogurt for a light-tasting alternative.

Classic hummus

The timings on cooking chickpeas vary hugely – much will depend on their size and age; the older they are the longer they tend to cook. Customise this basic recipe to suit your tastes: add more tahini, less lemon juice or finely chopped garlic as you prefer. See page 24 for additional tips.

1 Drain the soaked chickpeas and add to a large pan. Pour in the measured water then stir in the bicarbonate of soda and slowly bring to the boil.

2 Skim off any scum with a spoon then half cover the top of the pan with a lid and simmer for 45–75 minutes until the chickpeas are soft and can be pressed between two fingers.

3 Drain the chickpeas into a colander, reserving the cooking water for later, loosely cover the colander with a clean dish towel and leave the chickpeas to cool for 30 minutes.

4 Add the chickpeas to a food processor and spoon in 30ml/ 2 tbsp of tahini. Add the lemon juice and a little salt and cayenne pepper. Blitz for 2–3 minutes until finely blended.

5 Gradually mix in enough of the reserved cooking water or fresh water if preferred to give a smooth spoonable hummus – usually about 125ml/4fl oz/½ cup. Taste and adjust with extra tahini and seasoning if needed.

6 Spoon into a shallow bowl, swirl with the back of a spoon then drizzle with olive oil and sprinkle with the paprika. Serve with warm pitta bread or other accompaniment.

COOK'S TIP Keep an eye on the chickpeas as they cook, as you want to maintain a steady, even heat. While it is tempting to cover the pan completely, it will always boil over, so keep the lid half on and half off the pan.

SERVES 6–8

Makes 525g/1lb 5oz/2 cups
Prep 15 minutes
Soak overnight
Cook 45–75 minutes

200g/7oz/1 cup dried chickpeas, soaked overnight in cold water
2 litres/3½ pints/8 cups water
2.5ml/½ tsp bicarbonate of soda (baking soda)
30–60ml/2–4 tbsp tahini
Juice of 1 lemon
Salt and cayenne pepper

To finish
30ml/2 tbsp olive oil
Little sweet paprika

Energy 152kcal/635kJ; Protein 7.1g; Carbohydrate 12.5g, of which sugars 0.7g; Fat 8.5g, of which saturates 1.2g; Cholesterol 0mg; Calcium 64mg; Fibre 0.8g; Sodium 11mg.

Hot buttered hummus with garlic

Popular in Turkey, this hummus is served hot. Dip through the garlicky buttery juices to the creamy smooth hummus below for a truly wonderful style of hummus.

1 Drain the soaked chickpeas into a colander and add to a large pan. Pour in the measured water then stir in the bicarbonate of soda and slowly bring to the boil.

2 Skim off any scum with a spoon then half cover with a lid and simmer for 45–75 minutes or until the chickpeas are soft but still hold their shape well.

3 Drain the chickpeas into a colander set over a bowl and reserve the cooking water for later.

4 Heat the butter in a frying pan or skillet, add the garlic and cumin and cook for 2–3 minutes until the garlic is just beginning to colour.

5 Add three-quarters of the chickpeas to the bowl of a food processor, and pour over two-thirds of the butter. Add the remaining chickpeas to the garlic butter in the pan and fry for 4–5 minutes until just beginning to brown.

6 Meanwhile, add the lemon juice, tahini and a little salt and pepper to the food processor. Blitz until smooth. Adjust the consistency of the hummus with some of the reserved cooking water to make a smooth spoonable mixture and add more salt and cayenne pepper if needed.

7 Spoon the hot hummus into a shallow bowl, swirl the top with the back of a spoon then spoon over the hot garlicky chickpeas from the pan. Serve immediately.

SERVES 6

Makes 625g/1lb 7oz/
2½ cups
Prep 15 minutes
Soak overnight
Cook 50–80 minutes

200g/7oz/1 cup dried chickpeas, soaked overnight in cold water

2 litre/3½ pints/8 cups water

2.5ml/½ tsp bicarbonate of soda (baking soda)

75g/3oz butter

4 garlic cloves, thinly sliced

5ml/1 tsp cumin seeds, roughly crushed

Juice of ½ lemon

30ml/2 tbsp tahini

Salt and cayenne pepper

Energy 228kcal/953kJ; Protein 8.6g; Carbohydrate 16.6g, of which sugars 1g; Fat 14.6g, of which saturates 7g; Cholesterol 27mg; Calcium 19mg; Fibre 0g; Sodium 89mg.

Hummus with roasted butternut squash

SERVES 6

Makes 600g/1lb 6oz/
2¼ cups
Prep 20 minutes
Soak overnight
Cook 45–75 minutes

100g/3¾oz/½ cup dried
chickpeas, soaked overnight
in cold water

1 litre/1¾ pints/4 cups water,
plus 60ml/4 tbsp/¼ cup extra

1.5ml/¼ tsp bicarbonate of
soda (baking soda)

600g/1lb 6oz or ½ butternut
squash, cut into thick slices,
deseeded, peeled and cut
into 1cm/½in cubes

5ml/1 tsp fennel seeds,
roughly crushed

2.5ml/½ tsp turmeric

2.5ml/½ tsp sweet paprika

30ml/2 tbsp olive oil

15ml/1 tbsp tahini

1cm/½in piece root ginger,
peeled and sliced

1 garlic clove, sliced

30ml/2 tbsp 0% fat Greek (US
strained plain) yogurt

Salt and cayenne pepper

Tinged golden yellow with the addition of butternut squash in the hummus and in the topping, this is a very moreish hummus. It could be topped with grilled mackerel fillets or chicken breast to make a main meal.

1 Drain the soaked chickpeas into a colander then tip into a pan. Pour in the water and stir in the bicarbonate of soda. Bring the water slowly to the boil, skim off the scum with a spoon then half cover with a lid and simmer for 45–75 minutes or until the chickpeas are soft.

2 Meanwhile preheat the oven to 200°C/400°F/Gas 6. Add the butternut squash to a roasting pan, sprinkle with the fennel seeds, turmeric, paprika and a little salt then drizzle with the oil. Toss together then roast for 20–25 minutes until the squash is tinged brown.

3 Drain the cooked chickpeas into a colander, cover with a dish towel and leave to cool for 30 minutes.

4 Add the drained chickpeas to the bowl of a food processor with the tahini, ginger and garlic. Spoon in the yogurt, 30ml/ 2 tbsp of the extra water and half the roasted butternut squash. Blitz until smooth.

5 Taste and adjust the seasoning with extra salt, cayenne pepper and more water if needed. Spoon into a bowl and garnish with the rest of the roasted butternut squash. Serve with (bell) pepper and baby carrot dippers.

HEALTH NOTE Butternut squash is rich in beta-carotene which is also found in other vibrantly coloured vegetables such as carrots, red peppers, spinach and kale. This is converted by the body into vitamin A which is needed for normal cell division and growth and is vital to maintain good eye health. Beta-carotene is also an important antioxidant which may help to protect against cancer.

Energy 139kcal/588kJ; Protein 5.6g; Carbohydrate 17g, of which sugars 5.3g; Fat 5.9g, of which saturates 0.8g; Cholesterol 0mg; Calcium 64mg; Fibre 2.1g; Sodium 14mg.

Aubergine and harissa hummus

Traditionally aubergines would have been cooked in the dying embers of an open fire or barbecue for the most wonderful smoky flavour. If you have a gas hob then you can cook the whole aubergine directly on a low flame, but grilling makes for a much easier and just as tasty alternative.

1 Drain the soaked chickpeas into a colander then tip into a pan. Pour in the water then stir in the bicarbonate of soda. Slowly bring to the boil, skim off any scum with a spoon then half cover with a lid and simmer for 45–75 minutes or until the chickpeas are soft.

2 Meanwhile prick either end of the aubergine two or three times with a fork then cook on a piece of foil on the base of the grill or broiling pan under a preheated grill, for about 15 minutes, turning until the skin is blackened and charred and the centre is soft. Set aside to cool.

3 Drain the cooked chickpeas into a colander, cover with a dish towel and leave to cool for 30 minutes.

4 Cut the aubergine in half lengthways then peel off the charred skin. Add the soft flesh to the bowl of a food processor. Tip in the chickpeas then add 5ml/1 tsp harissa and 30ml/2 tbsp oil, the garlic, tahini, 30ml/2 tbsp fresh water and salt and cayenne pepper. Blitz together until smooth.

5 Taste and adjust the seasoning and add more fresh water if needed. Blitz again until very smooth. Spoon into a bowl, and swirl the top with the back of a spoon.

6 Mix the remaining harissa into the remaining oil, drizzle over the top and sprinkle with the toasted pine nuts and pomegranate seeds. Serve with red (bell) pepper, red onion and warm flatbread dippers.

SERVES 4–6

Makes 475g/17oz/2 cups
Prep 20 minutes
Soak overnight
Cook 45–75 minutes

100g/3¾oz/½ cup dried chickpeas, soaked in cold water overnight

1 litre/1¾ pints/4 cups water, plus 30–90ml/2–6 tbsp extra

1.5ml/¼ tsp bicarbonate of soda (baking soda)

350g/12oz/1 large aubergine (eggplant)

7.5ml/1½ tsp harissa paste

45ml/3 tbsp olive oil

1 garlic clove, sliced

15ml/1 tbsp tahini

Salt and cayenne pepper

To finish

10ml/2 tsp pine nuts, lightly toasted

Few pomegranate seeds

Energy 126kcal/529kJ; Protein 4.8g; Carbohydrate 9.7g, of which sugars 1.7g; Fat 7.9g, of which saturates 1.1g; Cholesterol 0mg; Calcium 15mg; Fibre 1.7g; Sodium 8mg.

Garlicky spinach hummus

SERVES 4

Makes 400g/14oz/1¾ cups
Prep 20 minutes
Soak overnight
Cook 45–75 minutes

100g/3¾oz/½ cup dried chickpeas, soaked in cold water overnight

1 litre/1¾ pint/4 cups water, plus 60–90ml/4–6 tbsp extra

1.5ml/¼ tsp bicarbonate of soda (baking soda)

15ml/1 tbsp tahini

1 garlic clove, sliced

Juice of ½ lemon

50g/2oz/2 cups baby spinach leaves

Salt and cayenne pepper

To finish
Few pomegranate seeds
Few baby spinach leaves

This eye-catching green hummus is packed with nutrients – vitamins, minerals, complex carbs to keep you energised, and protein for growth, repair and maintenance of every cell in your body.

1 Drain the soaked chickpeas into a colander then tip into a pan. Pour over the water and stir in the bicarbonate of soda. Slowly bring to the boil, skim off any scum with a spoon then half cover with a lid and simmer for 45–75 minutes or until the chickpeas are soft.

2 Drain the chickpeas into a colander, cover with a clean dish towel and leave to cool for 30 minutes.

3 Tip the chickpeas into the bowl of a food processor, and add the tahini, garlic, lemon juice and spinach leaves with 60ml/4 tbsp extra water and a little salt and cayenne pepper. Blitz until smooth.

4 Taste and adjust the seasoning and add extra water if needed. Blitz again until very smooth. Spoon into a bowl, then swirl the top with the back of a spoon.

5 Sprinkle with pomegranate seeds and baby spinach leaves and serve with bread sticks, see page 137, or warm flatbreads.

HEALTH NOTE Spinach is rich in carotenoids including beta-carotene and lutein which may help to protect against cancer, plus folates and potassium. Choose baby spinach leaves so that as much of the calcium and iron that the leaves contain may be absorbed by the body.

COOK'S TIP Spinach does go limp quickly, if you are buying loose from a farm shop, pack the leaves into a large plastic bag with a sprinkling of cold water, blow up the bag then seal with a clip tie and chill in the refrigerator to make a mini greenhouse.

Energy 104kcal/441kJ; Protein 6.7g; Carbohydrate 12.6g, of which sugars 0.9g; Fat 3.3g, of which saturates 0.4g; Cholesterol 0mg; Calcium 34mg; Fibre 0.4g; Sodium 27mg.

Hummus with walnut tarator

Creamy smooth homemade hummus is topped with the Turkish version of pesto sauce. Rather than making with pine nuts and parmesan, tarator is made with toasted walnuts, parsley, tahini, garlic and lemon. It is delicious with hummus but also complements grilled fish and barbecued chicken or beef too.

1 Drain the soaked chickpeas then tip into a pan. Pour in the water and stir in the bicarbonate of soda. Slowly bring the water to the boil, skim off any scum with a spoon then half cover with a lid and simmer for 45–75 minutes or until the chickpeas are soft.

2 Drain the chickpeas into a colander, cover with a clean dish towel and leave to cool for 30 minutes.

3 Add the chickpeas, tahini, lemon juice and salt and cayenne pepper to the bowl of a food processor. Blitz until smooth then gradually add about 60ml/4 tbsp cold water and blitz again.

4 Taste and adjust the seasoning and consistency with extra water if needed. Spoon into a shallow bowl and set aside.

5 To make the tarator sauce, dry-fry the walnut pieces for 2–3 minutes until lightly toasted. Cool for 10 minutes then add to the cleaned food processor bowl with the garlic, parsley and tahini. Blitz together until the nuts and parsley are finely chopped. Stir in the lemon juice, half the oil and a little salt and cayenne pepper.

6 Spoon a little of the tarator sauce over the hummus, drizzle with the remaining oil and sprinkle with a few extra nuts. Serve with a selection of mixed vegetable dippers and warm pitta bread dippers if you like.

SERVES 4

Makes 300g/11oz/
1⅓ cup hummus and
110g/4oz/generous ½ cup
tarator sauce
Prep 25 minutes
Soak overnight
Cook 45–75 minutes

100g/3¾oz/½ cups dried chickpeas, soaked overnight in cold water

1 litre/1¾ pint/4 cups water, plus 60–90ml/4–6 tbsp extra

1.5ml/¼ tsp bicarbonate of soda (baking soda)

15ml/1 tbsp tahini

Juice of ½ lemon

Salt and cayenne pepper

Tarator sauce

50g/2oz/⅓ cup walnut pieces, plus few extra for garnish

1 garlic clove, sliced

20g/¾oz/large handful fresh flat leaf parsley

10ml/2 tsp tahini

Juice of ½ lemon

30ml/2 tbsp olive oil

Salt and cayenne pepper

Energy 252kcal/1049kJ; Protein 8.8g; Carbohydrate 13g, of which sugars 1.1g; Fat 18.6g, of which saturates 2.2g; Cholesterol 0mg; Calcium 34mg; Fibre 0.9g; Sodium 12mg.

Tomato and smoked paprika hummus

Buy cherry tomatoes on the vine for that just-picked flavour. Cumin and smoked paprika-infused tomatoes make for a good marriage with the creamy smoothness of homemade hummus.

1 Drain the soaked chickpeas into a colander then tip into a pan. Pour in the water and stir in the bicarbonate of soda. Slowly bring the water to the boil, skim off the scum with a spoon then half cover with the lid and simmer for 45–75 minutes or until the chickpeas are soft.

2 Drain the chickpeas into a colander, cover with a clean dish towel and leave to cool for 30 minutes.

3 Meanwhile add the tomatoes to a frying pan or skillet, drizzle over 15ml/1 tbsp oil, sprinkle with the cumin seeds, paprika or chilli powder, and a little salt. Fry over a medium heat for 5 minutes until the tomatoes have softened.

4 Add the chickpeas, tahini, tomato purée and garlic to a food processor bowl. Blitz until smooth. Spoon in one third of the tomatoes and blitz again. Taste and adjust the seasoning and mix in 15–30ml/1–2 tbsp extra water, if needed.

5 Spoon the hummus into a shallow bowl, swirl the top with the back of a spoon then top with the remaining tomatoes, any pan juices and the remaining oil, and sprinkle with the paprika. Serve with warm bread and olives.

HEALTH NOTE Tomatoes are packed with antioxidant-rich vitamins A, C and E, and lycopene which is the carotene pigment that makes them red. They also contain the minerals zinc and selenium which are thought to help protect our body from free radical damage that may occur when you are feeling stressed or ill.

SERVES 4

Makes 400g/14oz/1¾ cups
Prep 20 minutes
Soak overnight
Cook 45–75 minutes

100g/3¾oz/½ cup dried chickpeas, soaked overnight in cold water

1 litre/1¾ pint/4 cups water, plus 15–30ml/1–2 tbsp extra

1.5ml/¼ tsp bicarbonate of soda (baking soda)

250g/9oz/about 14 cherry tomatoes, halved

30ml/2 tbsp olive oil

5ml/1 tsp cumin seeds, roughly crushed

1.5ml/¼ tsp hot smoked paprika or chilli powder, plus a little extra for sprinkling

15ml/1 tbsp tahini

5ml/1 tsp tomato purée (paste)

1 garlic clove, sliced

Salt and cayenne pepper

Energy 164kcal/687kJ; Protein 7g; Carbohydrate 14.8g, of which sugars 2.6g; Fat 8.9g, of which saturates 1.2g; Cholesterol 0mg; Calcium 17mg; Fibre 1g; Sodium 16mg.

Hummus with roasted onion

Slowly cooking onions with a little honey and crushed fennel seeds really brings out the flavour and adds a most wonderful caramelised taste, to complement the creamy smoothness of the hummus.

1 Drain the soaked chickpeas into a colander then tip into a pan. Pour in the water and stir in the bicarbonate of soda. Slowly bring the water to the boil, skim off the scum with a spoon then half cover with the lid and simmer for 45–75 minutes or until the chickpeas are soft.

2 Drain the chickpeas into a colander, cover with a clean dish towel and leave to cool for 30 minutes.

3 Meanwhile, heat the oil in a large frying pan, add the onions and fry over a medium heat for 10 minutes, stirring from time to time until softened and beginning to brown. Add the honey and fennel seeds and fry for 10–15 minutes more, stirring until the onions are caramelised.

4 Add the chickpeas, tahini and garlic to the bowl of a food processor. Add one-third of the onions, 15ml/1 tbsp of the lemon juice and 30ml/2 tbsp extra water and some salt and cayenne pepper. Blitz until smooth. Taste and adjust the seasoning, adding more lemon juice or salt and pepper if you like, then mix in more water if needed.

5 Spoon the hummus into a bowl, top with the remaining onions and serve with multiseed crispbreads or warm pitta bread.

HEALTH NOTE Onions are thought to have antibacterial and antiviral properties and may help us fight colds, flu, stomach viruses and candida yeast. They may even also help to reduce inflammation, which could be beneficial to those with arthritis.
COOK'S TIP If you don't have any fennel seeds then use cumin seeds.

SERVES 4

Makes 350g/12oz/1½ cups
Prep 20 minutes
Soak overnight
Cook 45–75 minutes

100g/3¾oz/½ cup dried chickpeas, soaked overnight in cold water

1 litre/1¾ pints/4 cups water, plus 30–60ml/2–4 tbsp extra

1.5ml/¼ tsp bicarbonate of soda (baking soda)

30ml/2 tbsp olive oil

250g/9oz/2 onions, halved and thinly sliced

5ml/1 tsp clear honey

5ml/1 tsp fennel seeds, roughly crushed

15ml/1 tbsp tahini

1 garlic clove, sliced

15–30ml/1–2 tbsp lemon juice

Salt and cayenne pepper

Energy 183kcal/765kJ; Protein 7.4g; Carbohydrate 19.5g, of which sugars 5.8g; Fat 8.9g, of which saturates 1.2g; Cholesterol 0mg; Calcium 29mg; Fibre 1.4g; Sodium 12mg.

Super-seedy hummus

SERVES 4

Makes 350g/12oz/1½ cups
Prep 20 minutes
Soak overnight
Cook 45–75 minutes

100g/3¾oz/½ cup dried
chickpeas, soaked overnight
in cold water
1 litre/1¾ pint/4 cups water,
plus 60ml/4 tbsp extra
1.5ml/¼ tsp bicarbonate of
soda (baking soda)
45ml/3 tbsp sunflower seeds
45ml/3 tbsp pumpkin seeds
10ml/2 tsp ground flaxseeds
1 garlic clove, sliced
15ml/1 tbsp tahini
25ml/1½ tbsp olive oil
Juice of ½ lemon
Salt and cayenne pepper
5ml/1 tsp clear honey
Little Gem (Bibb) lettuce
leaves, to serve

Lightly toasted seeds glazed with honey make a moreish topping and an additional protein boost to the hummus. Make up extra of the seed mix and add it to soups, muffins, and breakfast porridge.

1 Drain the soaked chickpeas into a colander then tip into a pan. Pour in the water and stir in the bicarbonate of soda. Bring the water to the boil, skim off the scum with a spoon then half cover with the lid and simmer for 45–75 minutes or until the chickpeas are soft.

2 Drain the chickpeas into a colander, cover with a clean dish towel and leave to cool for 30 minutes.

3 Add the chickpeas to a food processor bowl then add 15ml/1 tbsp of sunflower seeds and 15ml/1 tbsp pumpkin seeds and all the ground flaxseeds. Add the garlic, tahini, 15ml/1 tbsp of the oil, the lemon juice and a little salt and cayenne pepper. Blitz until smooth.

4 Taste and adjust the seasoning and add more water if needed. Blitz again until very smooth. Spoon into a bowl. Add the remaining oil to a frying pan then add the remaining seeds. Fry for 2 minutes over a medium heat then add the honey and cook for a minute or two more until just beginning to brown. To serve, spoon the hummus into Little Gem lettuce leaves and sprinkle with the remaining seeds.

HEALTH NOTE Seeds are a great way to boost protein for those who do not eat meat, and are an easy way to sneak in extra fibre, but they are high in calories. Pumpkin seeds contain iron, magnesium and zinc. Sunflower seeds contain vitamin C and useful amounts of linoleic acid. Flaxseeds (also called linseeds) are a good source of lignans, omega-3 and -6 fatty acids, plus magnesium.

Energy 293kcal/1222kJ; Protein 11.3g; Carbohydrate 18.6g, of which sugars 2.6g; Fat 19.6g, of which saturates 2.7g; Cholesterol 0mg; Calcium 40mg; Fibre 2g; Sodium 11mg.

Hummus with griddled peppers

Roasted peppers burst with flavour, and their bold colour tinges this hummus a deep orange. For a fiery finish drizzle with a little harissa paste mixed with a little extra olive oil.

1 Drain the soaked chickpeas into a colander then tip into a pan. Pour in the water and stir in the bicarbonate of soda. Slowly bring the water to the boil, skim off the scum with a spoon then half cover with the lid and simmer for 45–75 minutes or until the chickpeas are soft. Drain the chickpeas into a colander set over a bowl. Leave to cool for 30 minutes.

2 Meanwhile, line the grill or broiling pan with foil, tear the rosemary from the stem and scatter on top. Arrange the pepper quarters on top, skin-side up, drizzle with 15ml/1 tbsp of the oil and then grill for 10–15 minutes until the peppers are softened and the skins are charred and blackened. Wrap the foil around the peppers and leave to cool. Open out the foil, and lift the peppers off, reserving the cooking juices and rosemary. Peel the skins off the peppers then chop the flesh.

3 Add half the chopped peppers to the bowl of a food processor with all but a couple of spoonfuls of the chickpeas. Add the tahini, lemon juice and a little salt and cayenne pepper, and blitz until smooth. Taste and adjust the seasoning and add more water if needed. Blitz again until very smooth.

4 Spoon into a shallow bowl and swirl the top with the back of a spoon. Mix the remaining oil and rosemary cooking juices in a bowl, add the harissa if using, then stir in the remaining chopped peppers and chickpeas. Season with salt and spoon over the top of the hummus. Serve with warm bread or mixed vegetable dippers.

SERVES 4

Makes 400g/14oz/1¾ cups
Prep 20 minutes
Soak overnight
Cook 45–75 minutes

100g/3¾oz/½ cup dried chickpeas, soaked overnight in cold water

1 litre/1¾ pint/4 cups water, plus 60ml/4 tbsp extra

1.5ml/¼ tsp bicarbonate of soda (baking soda)

1 fresh rosemary stem

1 red (bell) pepper, quartered, cored and deseeded

1 orange (bell) pepper, quartered, cored and deseeded

30ml/2 tbsp olive oil

30ml/2 tbsp tahini

Juice of ½ lemon

Salt and cayenne pepper

5ml/1 tsp harissa paste, optional

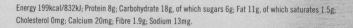

Energy 199kcal/832kJ; Protein 8g; Carbohydrate 18g, of which sugars 6g; Fat 11g, of which saturates 1.5g; Cholesterol 0mg; Calcium 20mg; Fibre 1.9g; Sodium 13mg.

Triple nut hummus

SERVES 4

Makes 375g/13oz/scant
1¾ cups
Prep 20 minutes
Soak overnight
Cook 45–75 minutes

100g/3¾oz/½ cup dried
chickpeas, soaked overnight
in cold water

1 litre/1¾ pints/4 cups water
plus 60–90ml/4–6 tbsp extra

1.5ml/¼ tsp bicarbonate of
soda (baking soda)

25g/1oz butter

20g/¾oz/2 tbsp pine nuts

25g/1oz/2 tbsp unblanched
almonds, roughly chopped

25g/1oz/2 tbsp pistachio
nuts, roughly chopped

1 garlic clove, sliced

Juice of ½ lemon

Salt and cayenne pepper

Not everyone is a fan of sesame seed tahini. By frying pistachio, almonds and pine nuts in a little butter and blending with home-cooked chickpeas you get a hummus that is just as rich in flavour, with a creamy smoothness and a delicious crunchy buttery topping.

1 Drain the soaked chickpeas into a colander then tip into a pan. Pour in the water then stir in the bicarbonate of soda. Slowly bring to the boil, skim off any scum with a spoon then half cover with a lid and simmer for 45–75 minutes or until the chickpeas are soft. Drain the chickpeas into a colander, cover with a clean dish towel and leave to cool for 15 minutes until still just warm.

2 Heat half of the butter in a frying pan or skillet, add the nuts and fry over a medium heat, stirring for 3–4 minutes until golden brown and toasted.

3 Add the drained chickpeas, half the fried nuts, the garlic and lemon juice to the bowl of a food processor. Add 60ml/ 4 tbsp extra water and a little salt and cayenne pepper. Blitz together until smooth. Adjust the seasoning and add extra water if needed. Blitz again until very smooth.

4 Spoon into a bowl, and swirl the top with the back of a spoon. Add the rest of the butter to the remaining nuts, warm until the butter is foaming then spoon over the top of the hummus. Serve with warm bread and vegetable dippers.

HEALTH NOTE Protein-boosting nuts add crunch if roughly chopped or creaminess if finely ground. They are quite high in fat, but it is the good kind, unsaturated fat, which gives us energy, although fat of any kind does ramp up the calories so eat in small quantities and try to avoid grazing on a bowl of nuts.
COOK'S TIP You could just add 50g/2oz/5 tbsp pine nuts instead of the mix of nuts if preferred.

Energy 248kcal/1033kJ; Protein 8.2g; Carbohydrate 13.1g, of which sugars 1.4g; Fat 18.5g, of which saturates 4.2g; Cholesterol 13mg; Calcium 16mg; Fibre 0.5g; Sodium 48mg.

Hummus with herb oil

You don't need lots of ingredients to make a dish taste good, just a few quality ones. Summery herbs and olive oil make this hummus extra special. The herb oil can also be drizzled over hot soups or tossed with pasta and some toasted walnuts.

1 Drain the soaked chickpeas into a colander then tip into a pan. Pour in the water then stir in the bicarbonate of soda. Slowly bring to the boil, skim off any scum with a spoon then half cover with a lid and simmer for 45–75 minutes or until the chickpeas are soft.

2 Meanwhile, finely chop the herbs. Heat the oil in a small frying pan, take off the heat, stir in the herbs and leave to infuse while the chickpeas cook.

3 Drain the chickpeas into a colander set over a bowl, cover with a clean dish towel and leave to cool for 30 minutes.

4 Add the drained chickpeas, tahini, garlic and lemon juice to the bowl of a food processor. Add 60ml/4 tbsp water and a little salt and cayenne pepper. Blitz until smooth.

5 Adjust the seasoning and add extra water if needed. Blitz again until very smooth. Spoon half the herb oil into the hummus and very lightly stir together for a marbled effect. Spoon into a bowl and swirl the rest of the herb oil on top. Serve with baby lettuce, peeled cucumber pieces and sliced baby fennel dippers.

HEALTH NOTE The Mediterranean diet has long been thought of as the ideal healthy diet. Rich in vegetables, olive oil and grains with red wine in moderation. The key is to get a wide range of different foods and keep those foods high in sugar as a treat.

SERVES 4

Makes 350g/12oz/1½ cups
Prep 20 minutes
Soak overnight
Cook 45–75 minutes

100g/3¾oz/½ cup dried chickpeas, soaked overnight in cold water

1 litre/1¾ pints/4 cups water plus 60–90ml/4–6 tbsp extra

1.5ml/¼ tsp bicarbonate of soda (baking soda)

15g/½oz/1 large handful fresh coriander (cilantro)

15g/½oz/1 large handful fresh flat leaf parsley

60ml/4 tbsp olive oil

15ml/1 tbsp tahini

1 garlic clove, sliced

Juice of ½ lemon

Salt and cayenne pepper

Energy 203kcal/845kJ; Protein 6.6g; Carbohydrate 12.6g, of which sugars 0.8g; Fat 14.3g, of which saturates 1.9g; Cholesterol 0mg; Calcium 28mg; Fibre 0.5g; Sodium 12mg.

Whipped hummus with yogurt

SERVES 4

Makes 400g/14oz/1¾ cups
Prep 20 minutes
Soak overnight
Cook 45–75 minutes

100g/3¾oz/½ cup dried chickpeas, soaked overnight in cold water

1 litre/1¾ pints/4 cups water

1.5ml/¼ tsp bicarbonate of soda (baking soda)

125g/4¼oz/½ cup fat-free Greek (US strained plain) yogurt

Juice of ½ lemon

20ml/4 tsp tahini

Salt and cayenne pepper

To finish

15ml/1 tbsp fat-free Greek (US strained plain) yogurt

Few black and green herb-marinated olives

Little sweet paprika

Creamy smooth and light-tasting, this version of hummus is made with fat-free Greek yogurt and tangy lemon juice for a summery feel. Try in sandwiches, with salad, or swirled over a plate and topped with barbecued prawns or chicken.

1 Drain the soaked chickpeas into a colander then tip into a pan. Pour in the water and stir in the bicarbonate of soda. Slowly bring to the boil, skim off any scum with a spoon then half cover with a lid and simmer for 45–75 minutes or until the chickpeas are soft.

2 Drain the chickpeas into a colander set over a bowl. Cover with a clean dish towel and leave to cool for 30 minutes.

3 Add the chickpeas to the bowl of a food processor, spoon in the yogurt, lemon juice and tahini, then season with a little salt and cayenne pepper. Blitz until smooth.

4 Adjust the seasoning if needed then spoon into a bowl. Top with extra yogurt, the olives and sprinkle with a little paprika. Serve with triangles of warm flatbread for dipping.

HEALTH NOTE Probiotic yogurts are thought to increase good bacteria in the gut to aid digestion, but these microscopic bacteria created by fermenting milk to make yogurt are heat–sensitive and can be lost by pasteurisation, so not all yogurt on the supermarket shelves will contain them. Choose brands that say on the back of the pack 'live active cultures'. As Greek yogurt is strained it is thicker and creamier with more protein and a lower lactose content than ordinary yogurt.

COOK'S TIP Tahini is quick and easy to make at home with sesame seeds and just a little oil, so if you run out or you can't find it in your nearest store, see pages 22–3 on how to make.

Energy 127kcal/537kJ; Protein 8.5g; Carbohydrate 15.3g, of which sugars 3.4g; Fat 3.9g, of which saturates 0.5g; Cholesterol 0mg; Calcium 69mg; Fibre 0g; Sodium 35mg.

HUMMUS WITH A TWIST

While purists will say hummus should only be made with home-cooked chickpeas, modern cooks often favour the convenience of canned chickpeas. These recipes use canned chickpeas but you can of course use home-soaked and cooked ones! Push the boundaries even further and try homemade hummus with red kidney beans, black beans, mung beans, even frozen broad beans.

No-cook hummus

SERVES 4

Makes 350g/12oz/1½ cups
Prep 5 minutes

400g/14oz can chickpeas in
water, drained
30ml/2 tbsp tahini
Juice of ½ lemon
45–60ml/3–4 tbsp cold water
Salt and cayenne pepper

To finish
10ml/2 tsp olive oil
Little sweet paprika or
sprinkling of sumac seeds

While home-cooked chickpeas are the base of truly
authentic hummus, there are just some moments when
time is against you. This easy version is made with canned
chickpeas for speed; just add everything to a food
processor and blitz. What could be easier or quicker.

1 Reserve a few of the drained chickpeas for garnish and add
the rest to the bowl of a food processor. Add the tahini,
lemon juice, 45ml/3 tbsp water and a little salt and cayenne
pepper and blitz until smooth.

2 Taste and adjust with extra seasoning and more water if
needed. Blitz again until very smooth.

3 Spoon into a bowl and swirl the top with the back of a
spoon. Top with the reserved chickpeas, the olive oil and a
little paprika or sumac seeds. Serve with (bell) pepper, carrot
and cucumber sticks and a few baby lettuce leaves.

HEALTH NOTE Encouraging the family to dunk into hummus with
a mix of raw dippers or crudités is an easy way to boost vegetable
intakes and makes a much healthier snack than munching on high-
salt crisps and other processed snacks.

COOK'S TIP Tahini can be bought in jars and is available in
two types, choose 'light' tahini for hummus. Or have a go
at making your own; it is incredibly easy to make in a
food processor or liquidiser, see pages 22–3 for details.

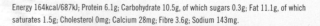

Energy 164kcal/687kJ; Protein 6.1g; Carbohydrate 10.5g, of which sugars 0.3g; Fat 11.1g, of which
saturates 1.5g; Cholesterol 0mg; Calcium 28mg; Fibre 3.6g; Sodium 143mg.

Hummus with buttery za'atar

Butter might not seem like an obvious choice to drizzle over hummus but it adds a luxurious richness. Serve immediately while the butter is still warm.

1 Heat the butter in a pan until foaming then stir in the za'atar spice mix. Reserve a few chickpeas for garnish and add the rest to the bowl of a food processor with half the za'atar butter.

2 Add the tahini, garlic, lemon juice and 60ml/4 tbsp boiling water. Season with salt and cayenne pepper. Blitz until smooth. Taste and adjust with extra seasoning and more water if needed. Blitz again until very smooth.

3 Spoon into a bowl and swirl the top with the back of a spoon. Warm the remaining za'atar butter with the reserved chickpeas. Spoon over the hummus and serve immediately with warm flatbreads or pitta breads.

HEALTH NOTE Butter is no longer seen as the baddie when compared with margarine; they both have a similar fat content and provide the same amount of energy, unless the margarine is labelled a low-fat or reduced-fat version. We need fat in our body for energy and to cushion our vital organs, plus butter contains fat-soluble vitamins A and D. The key is to eat saturated fat in moderation.
COOK'S TIP Not a fan of garlic? Simply leave it out.

SERVES 4

Makes 350g/12oz/1½ cups
Prep 10 minutes
Cook 2 minutes

25g/1oz butter

10ml/2 tsp za'atar spice mix, see page 29

400g/14oz can chickpeas in water, drained

30ml/2 tbsp tahini

1 garlic clove, sliced

Juice of ½ lemon

60–90ml/4–6 tbsp boiling water

Salt and cayenne pepper

Energy 161kcal/675kJ; Protein 6.6g; Carbohydrate 10.5g, of which sugars 0.3g; Fat 11.2g, of which saturates 4g; Cholesterol 13mg; Calcium 53mg; Fibre 3.6g; Sodium 185mg.

Spiced carrot and cumin hummus

SERVES 6

**Makes 550g/1lb 4oz/
2¾ cups
Prep 10 minutes
Cook 2–3 minutes**

30ml/2 tbsp olive oil
100g/3¾oz/1 medium carrot,
coarsely grated
2.5ml/½ tsp cumin seeds,
roughly crushed
2.5ml/½ tsp coriander seeds,
roughly crushed
400g/14oz can chickpeas in
water, drained
30ml/2 tbsp tahini
30ml/2 tbsp 0% fat Greek
(US strained plain) yogurt
Juice of ½ lemon
60–90ml/4–6 tbsp water
Salt and cayenne pepper
Little sweet paprika

An easy way to sneak some extra vegetables into this tasty hummus without the kids realising.

1 Heat 15ml/1 tbsp oil in a frying pan, add the carrot and seeds and cook for 2–3 minutes, stirring until just softened. Add the carrot mix to the bowl of a food processor with the chickpeas, tahini, yogurt, lemon juice, 60ml/4 tbsp water, salt and cayenne pepper. Blitz until smooth.

2 Taste and adjust the seasoning and add extra water if needed. Blitz again until very smooth. Spoon into a bowl, swirl the top with the back of a spoon, drizzle with the remaining oil and sprinkle with a little paprika. Serve with pitta crisps, see below, or vegetable dippers.

PITTA CRISPS Don't throw away pitta breads which are a little past their best; either sprinkle with water and grill or broil until puffed up or cut them into squares and put on to a sheet of oiled foil set on a baking sheet, drizzle with a little more olive oil and sprinkle with za'atar spice mix. Bake for 5–10 minutes in a preheated oven set to 180°C/350°F/Gas 4 until crisp and brown around the edges.

Energy 118kcal/494kJ; Protein 4.4g; Carbohydrate 8.7g, of which sugars 1.8g; Fat 7.5g, of which saturates 1g; Cholesterol 0mg; Calcium 31mg; Fibre 2.9g; Sodium 103mg.

Beetroot and borlotti bean hummus

Flavoured with za'atar, a popular Middle Eastern spice mix made of thyme, oregano, sumac and sesame seeds, this fabulous deep red, exotic-looking hummus is packed with good carbs to help fight fatigue and boost energy. And it's no-cook too!

1 Add the beetroot and drained beans to the bowl of a food processor, sprinkle in the za'atar and paprika then add the tahini and garlic. Season and blitz until finely chopped.

2 Pour in the lemon juice and 60ml/4 tbsp water, and blitz again until smooth. Taste and adjust the seasoning and water if needed then blitz again until very smooth.

3 Spoon into a bowl, swirl with the back of a spoon then drizzle the oil over the top and sprinkle with a little extra za'atar. Serve with red-tipped chicory (Belgian endive) dippers if you want to enhance the all-red effect.

HEALTH NOTE Beetroot is packed with nutrients and antioxidants. The pigment beta-cyanin gives beetroot its amazing colour and works with manganese and vitamin C to aid good eye health and overall good tissue health. It is rich in other minerals too, plus folates for new cell growth and DNA important for pregnant women. Beetroot may even help reduce the oxidation of LDL cholesterol, so helping to reduce the risk of heart disease.

COOK'S TIP The same weight of cooked beetroot could also be used in place of the raw, but choose beetroot that are vacuum-packed in natural juices rather than vinegar.

SERVES 6

**Makes 525g/1lb 5oz/
scant 2½ cups
Prep 15 minutes**

150g/5oz trimmed beetroot
(beet), about 2, scrubbed
and cut into chunks

400g/14oz can borlotti beans
in water, drained

5ml/1 tsp za'atar spice mix,
see page 29

5ml/1 tsp sweet paprika

15ml/1 tbsp tahini

1 garlic clove, sliced

Juice of ½ lemon

60–90ml/4–6 tbsp cold water

Salt and cayenne pepper

To finish
15ml/1 tbsp olive oil
Little extra za'atar spice mix

Energy 87kcal/366kJ; Protein 4.1g; Carbohydrate 10.2g, of which sugars 3.3g; Fat 3.6g, of which saturates 0.5g; Cholesterol 0mg; Calcium 39mg; Fibre 4.2g; Sodium 186mg.

White bean and feta hummus

Speckled with fresh mint, parsley and garlic, this delicious and very moreish feta-flavoured hummus tastes great spread on warmed flat bread, or try it layered in jars with shredded salad leaves and grated carrot and beetroot for a healthy energy-packed lunch on the go.

1 Add the drained beans to the bowl of a food processor. Reserve one quarter of the feta cheese then crumble the rest into the beans. Add the garlic, oil and lemon juice and blitz until smooth.

2 Tear the mint and parsley leaves from the stems and add to the hummus with the water and some salt and cayenne pepper. Blitz again then adjust with extra water and more seasoning if needed and blitz until very smooth.

3 Spoon into a bowl, and swirl the top with the back of a spoon. Drizzle with extra olive oil, sprinkle with the remaining feta, crumbled into small pieces, and garnish with some chopped parsley, tiny mint leaves and a sprinkle of paprika. Serve with (bell) pepper strips and warm focaccia breads.

HEALTH NOTE Feta cheese can be made with sheep or cows' milk and is packed with protein and fat–soluble vitamins A and D, plus vitamin B12 to help with brain function. However it does have higher salt levels than some other cheeses. When seasoning the hummus add just a small amount of salt, less than for other hummus recipes, and taste as you go. World Health Organisation guidelines recommend that we should only consume 6g or around 1 tsp of salt a day.

COOK'S TIP Grow parsley and mint in pots by the back door for an aromatic herby addition to hummus, salads and stews.

SERVES 4

Makes 400g/14oz/1¾ cups
Prep 10 minutes

400g/14oz can cannellini beans in water, drained
100g/3¾oz feta cheese, drained
1 garlic clove, sliced
30ml/2 tbsp olive oil
Juice of ½ lemon
3 stems fresh mint
3 stems fresh flat leaf parsley
30ml/2 tbsp water
Salt and cayenne pepper

To finish
15ml/1 tbsp olive oil
Little roughly chopped fresh flat leaf parsley
Few tiny fresh mint leaves
Sprinkle of paprika

Energy 204kcal/850kJ; Protein 8.6g; Carbohydrate 12.2g, of which sugars 2.9g; Fat 13.8g, of which saturates 4.7g; Cholesterol 18mg; Calcium 151mg; Fibre 5.9g; Sodium 616mg.

Garlicky kale and lemon hummus

Kale may not be an obvious choice for adding to hummus but this trendy, nutrient-rich vegetable adds lutein and zeaxanthin, two powerful cancer-fighting antioxidants, plus it helps to boost vitamins C, K, chlorophyll and iron which helps to fight fatigue.

1 Add the drained chickpeas, kale, parsley and garlic to the bowl of a food processor. Add the tahini and then pour in the lemon juice.

2 Blitz until smooth then add 60ml/4 tbsp water and a little salt and cayenne pepper. Blitz until smooth. Taste and adjust the seasoning and consistency with a little extra water, if needed. Blitz again until very smooth.

3 Spoon into a bowl, swirl the top with the back of a spoon and garnish with a little extra shredded kale and parsley, and a sprinkling of black pepper, if liked. Serve with veggie dippers and warm lavash, see page 134, or warmed pitta breads.

HEALTH NOTE Lemons are a rich source of vitamin C which helps to boost immunity and fight infection. This vitamin cannot be stored by the body and is heat sensitive. Stirring it into hummus is an easy way to boost this vital vitamin for those members of the family who are not keen on fruit.

COOK'S TIP Kale can be bought ready shredded from the supermarket or look out for whole leaves from your local farmer's market or farm shop. Bright green curly kale, sometimes called Scotch kale, is the most common; red Russian kale has softer larger frilled leaves while the Italian cavolo nero, often called black kale, adds a much darker tone to hummus.

SERVES 4–5

Makes 425g/15oz/ scant 2 cups
Prep 10 minutes

400g/14oz can chickpeas in water, drained

25g/1oz/generous 1 cup shredded kale

3 stems fresh parsley, leaves torn from stems

1 garlic clove, sliced

30ml/2 tbsp tahini

Juice of 1 lemon

60–75ml/4–5 tbsp water

Salt and cayenne pepper

To finish
Little extra shredded kale and chopped fresh parsley
Little ground black pepper

Energy 98kcal/411kJ; Protein 5g; Carbohydrate 8.5g, of which sugars 0.3g; Fat 5.1g, of which saturates 0.7g; Cholesterol 0mg; Calcium 70mg; Fibre 3.7g; Sodium 118mg.

Smoky corn and white bean hummus

SERVES 6

**Makes 475g/15oz/
scant 2 cups
Prep 10 minutes
Cook 20 minutes**

1 corn on the cob, trimmed
of leaves

1.5ml/¼ tsp hot smoked
paprika

1.5ml/¼ tsp ground cumin

5ml/1 tsp tomato purée
(paste)

15ml/1 tbsp sunflower or
olive oil

2 spring onions (scallions),
roughly chopped

400g/14oz can cannellini
beans, drained

Handful fresh coriander
(cilantro) leaves

15ml/1 tbsp tahini

15ml/1 tbsp shelled hemp
seeds

Juice of ½ lemon

30–45ml/2–3 tbsp cold water

Salt and cayenne pepper

Little paprika, to garnish

Baking corn cobs in the oven with smoked paprika adds a spicy heat that tastes great when mixed with healthy beans, zingy coriander leaves and spring onions in this unusual and healthy hummus.

1 Preheat the oven to 180°C/350°F/Gas 4. Put the corn on a piece of foil then mix the smoked paprika, cumin, tomato purée and oil together and brush over the corn. Wrap the foil around the corn to enclose completely then put the parcel on a baking sheet and cook in the oven for 20 minutes until tender. Leave to cool.

2 Open the foil parcel and cut the corn niblets away from the central core with a knife. Reserve a few niblets and a little chopped green spring onion for garnish and add the rest to a food processor bowl with the drained beans, fresh coriander, spring onions, tahini and hemp seeds. Blitz until finely chopped.

3 Pour in the lemon juice, add 30ml/2 tbsp water and a little salt and cayenne pepper then blitz until smooth. Taste and adjust the seasoning and add a little extra water if needed.

4 Spoon into a bowl and garnish with the reserved corn and spring onion and a little paprika. Serve with crispbreads or tortilla chips.

HEALTH NOTE Naturally sweet, corn is packed with complex carbohydrates, or good carbs, including fibre to provide a stable and slow release of energy and small amounts of protein and potassium. It also contains two important phytochemicals, lutein and zeaxanthin, that promote healthy vision. The fresher the corn cobs the better nutritionally they are, and when they are really fresh the corn should be juicy, not dry when pierced.

COOK'S TIP Smoked paprika adds a great smoky barbecue flavour. If you don't have any then use chilli powder instead in this recipe.

Energy 105kcal/442kJ; Protein 4.7g; Carbohydrate 13.5g, of which sugars 2.3g; Fat 4g, of which saturates 0.5g; Cholesterol 0mg; Calcium 33mg; Fibre 4.3g; Sodium 170mg.

Chilli red bean hummus

Awaken the tastebuds with this hot and fiery hummus. The heat is cumulative, so don't be tempted to add extra chilli until you have tried a few mouthfuls first.

1 Add the oil, garlic, dried chillies and cumin to a small frying pan and cook over a low heat for 3 minutes to bring out the flavours. Take off the heat, stir in the paprika and leave to cool.

2 Tip the kidney beans into the bowl of a food processor, add the tahini, half the chilli oil mix and a little salt. Spoon in the water then blitz until smooth. Taste and adjust the seasoning and add extra water, if needed.

3 Spoon the hummus into a shallow bowl, swirl the top with the back of a spoon then drizzle over the remaining chilli oil and garnish with the sun-dried tomatoes and a little extra dried chilli. Serve with bread sticks, see page 137.

COOK'S TIP Dried red kidney beans could be used in place of the canned: soak 100g/3¾oz/½ cup in cold water overnight then drain, and add to a pan with 1 litre/1¾ pints/4 cups of water. Bring to the boil and then, very importantly, boil rapidly for 10 minutes, before reducing the heat and simmering until soft. These are the only dried pulses that must be boiled in this way to destroy harmful levels of toxins.

SERVES 4

Makes 365g/12½oz/
generous 1½ cups
Prep 10 minutes
Cook 3 minutes

45ml/3 tbsp olive oil
2 garlic cloves, thinly sliced
5ml/1 tsp dried crushed red chillies, plus extra to garnish
2.5ml/½ tsp cumin seeds, roughly crushed
5ml/1 tsp sweet paprika
400g/14oz can red kidney beans in water, drained, rinsed with cold water and drained again
15ml/1 tbsp tahini
Salt
60ml/4 tbsp/¼ cup water

To finish
25g/1oz/4 pieces drained sun-dried tomatoes in oil, roughly chopped

Energy 222kcal/923kJ; Protein 5.8g; Carbohydrate 12.8g, of which sugars 2.5g; Fat 16.8g, of which saturates 2.4g; Cholesterol 0mg; Calcium 53mg; Fibre 5.4g; Sodium 317mg.

Mixed bean and tuna hummus

Chickpeas are a good source of protein but here they get an extra boost with that favourite larder standby, a can of tuna. Lovely served as a dip, but try as a topping to a baked jacket potato too.

1 Chop a little of the coriander, red pepper and spring onion and put into a bowl with a little of the tuna and a few of the canned beans. Sprinkle with the lemon zest and mix with 15ml/1 tbsp of the oil then set aside.

2 Add the rest of the coriander, red pepper, spring onion, tuna and beans to the bowl of a food processor. Spoon in the paprika, tomato purée, tahini, yogurt and remaining oil then season with salt and cayenne pepper. Blitz until smooth.

3 Taste and adjust the seasoning if needed. Spoon into a bowl then top with the diced red pepper and tuna mix. Serve with sugar snap peas, cucumber and celery stick dippers.

HEALTH NOTE Protein makes up the building blocks of our body. It is essential for growth, repair and maintenance of cells from muscles and bones to hair and fingernails as well as building hormones, enzymes and antibodies to help keep us in top condition.
COOK'S TIP Frozen ready-chopped herbs make a great standby for those days when you haven't been shopping, or keep supermarket growing pots of herbs longer by transplanting into a slightly larger pot when you get home and keeping on the kitchen windowsill.

SERVES 6

Makes 600g/1lb 6oz/2¾ cups
Prep 20 minutes

3 stems fresh coriander (cilantro)
40g/1½oz/1 red (bell) pepper from a jar of roasted red peppers in brine
2 spring onions (scallions), sliced
160g/5¼oz can tuna fish in water, drained weight 120g
400g/14oz can mixed beans in water, drained
Grated zest and juice of ½ lemon
30ml/2 tbsp olive oil
5ml/1 tsp sweet paprika
10ml/2 tsp tomato purée (paste)
30ml/2 tbsp tahini
30ml/2 tbsp 0% fat Greek (US strained plain) yogurt
Salt and cayenne pepper

Energy 93kcal/385kJ; Protein 5.2g; Carbohydrate 1.2g, of which sugars 1.1g; Fat 7.5g, of which saturates 1.1g; Cholesterol 10mg; Calcium 12mg; Fibre 0.3g; Sodium 72mg.

Black bean and black olive hummus

Packed with Mediterranean tastes, this unusually coloured hummus is infused with pesto and fresh basil for the most delicious flavour. You might also like to serve this with a roasted pepper salad, chargrilled or barbecued lamb skewers, or steak.

1 Drain the soaked beans and add to a pan with the water, bring to the boil and skim off any scum with a spoon. Cover with a lid and simmer for about 1 hour or until tender.

2 Drain the beans into a colander and leave for 15 minutes then tip into the bowl of a food processor. Mix 5ml/1 tsp of the pesto with 10ml/2 tsp olive oil in a small bowl then set aside. Add the rest of the pesto and oil to the food processor with three-quarters of the basil and three-quarters of the olives. Season with salt and cayenne pepper and blitz until smooth.

3 Taste and adjust the seasoning and add a little water if needed. Spoon into a shallow bowl, swirl with the back of a spoon and garnish with the reserved pesto oil, olives and tiny basil leaves. Serve with warm olive focaccia bread, celery and cucumber sticks.

HEALTH NOTE Cultivated for some 5,000 years, olives have long been grown in the Western Mediterranean and Middle East. There are even trees still standing that are as old as the first Bible and Koran texts. Olives contain healthy oils just like olive oil, plus small amounts of fibre, iron, calcium and vitamin A. 15ml/1 tbsp of olive oil contains 120 calories, while 4–5 olives around 45 calories.
COOK'S TIP For garlic fans, add 1 or 2 sliced garlic cloves to the food processor when blitzing the beans.

SERVES 4

Makes 400g/14oz/1¾ cups
Prep 15 minutes
Soak overnight
Cook 1 hour 10 minutes

100g/3¾oz/½ cup dried black beans, soaked overnight in cold water

1 litre/1¾ pint/4 cups water, plus 30–45ml/3–4 tbsp extra

20ml/4 tsp pesto

45ml/3 tbsp olive oil

Small handful fresh basil, plus some tiny leaves for garnish

110g/4oz/scant 1 cup pitted black Kalamata olives

Salt and cayenne pepper

Energy 205kcal/856kJ; Protein 7.1g; Carbohydrate 13.7g, of which sugars 0.7g; Fat 14g, of which saturates 1.8g; Cholesterol 2mg; Calcium 62mg; Fibre 3.8g; Sodium 640mg.

Broad bean and avocado hummus

SERVES 4

Makes 350g/12oz/1½ cups
Prep 15 minutes
Cook 4–5 minutes

175g/6oz/1 generous cup
frozen broad (fava) beans

1 small avocado, halved and
stoned (pitted)

Handful fresh coriander
(cilantro) leaves

1 spring onion (scallion),
roughly chopped

½–1 red chilli, halved,
deseeded and roughly
chopped

1.5ml/¼ tsp sumac seeds

Juice of 1 lime

45–60ml/3–4 tbsp cold water

Salt and cayenne pepper

To finish
Little sumac
Little extra finely chopped
red chilli

While hummus is traditionally made with dried chickpeas this quick and easy recipe uses frozen broad beans for a version that is cooked in under 5 minutes. The addition of creamy avocado adds a velvety smoothness with just a touch of chilli to awaken the tastebuds. While it may leave the purists raising their eyebrows, this hummus makes for a super speedy, tasty and healthy lunch.

1 Add the frozen broad beans to a pan of boiling water, bring the water back to the boil and simmer for 4–5 minutes until just tender. Drain into a colander and rinse with cold water to cool quickly.

2 Scoop the avocado flesh from the skin with a spoon, reserve one quarter for the garnish and add the rest to the bowl of a food processor. Tip in the broad beans then add the fresh coriander, spring onion, a little chilli and sumac seeds. Blitz until finely chopped.

3 Add the lime juice and 30ml/2 tbsp water along with a little salt and cayenne pepper. Blitz again until smooth. Taste and adjust the seasoning and add extra chilli and water if needed. Blitz again until very smooth. Spoon into a bowl, swirl the top with the back of a spoon and garnish with the reserved avocado, cut into dice, a little sumac and extra red chilli. Serve immediately with celery stick dippers.

HEALTH NOTE Rich in concentrated energy in the form of good monounsaturated fats plus vitamin B6 to aid energy release, avocados also contain more potassium than bananas, to help regulate blood pressure and lower the risk of heart attacks and strokes, and are rich in vitamin E with smaller amounts of vitamin C and lutein, all powerful antioxidants.

COOK'S TIP If you would rather use fresh broad beans when in season, then pod and use the same weight as frozen and cook until just tender; tiny beans will take a little less time and larger ones more.

Energy 86kcal/360kJ; Protein 4.2g; Carbohydrate 5.9g, of which sugars 0.9g; Fat 5.3g, of which saturates 1.1g; Cholesterol 0mg; Calcium 43mg; Fibre 5.5g; Sodium 8mg.

Summery green pea hummus

This hummus encapsulates everything about summer, being light, fresh and very green. Serve with griddled asparagus, baby carrots, red-tipped chicory leaves and warm flatbreads for a relaxed appetizer or light lunch.

1 Drain the soaked split peas and add to a pan with the water, bring to the boil and skim off any scum with a spoon. Half cover with a lid and simmer for about 1 hour or until tender.

2 Add the fresh or frozen peas to a steamer and set over the pan of simmering split peas, cover and cook for 5 minutes.

3 Drain the boiled split peas into a sieve or strainer and leave to cool for 15 minutes then tip into the bowl of a food processor. Add the steamed fresh or frozen peas, the yogurt, herbs and lemon juice. Season with salt and cayenne pepper then blitz until smooth.

4 Taste and adjust with a little extra seasoning and a tablespoon or two of water, if needed. Spoon into a shallow bowl, swirl the top with the back of a spoon, and then add a drizzle of olive oil and some extra herb leaves, if liked. Serve with griddled vegetable dippers.

HEALTH NOTE Fresh or frozen green peas contain bone-building and osteoporosis-fighting vitamin K and manganese, plus folates which are micro-nutrients crucial for heart health and foetal development. The protein and fibre peas contain will leave you feeling fuller for longer than some other vegetables.
COOK'S TIP To griddle asparagus, rub trimmed stems with a little oil, sprinkle with coarse salt and cook on a preheated ridged pan for 2–3 minutes until hot, but still crunchy. Carrots take a few minutes more, chicory (Belgian endive) just 1 minute.

SERVES 4

Makes 400g/14oz/1¾ cups
Prep 20 minutes
Soak overnight
Cook 1 hour 5 minutes

100g/3¾oz/½ cup dried green split peas, soaked overnight in cold water

1 litre/1¾ pints/4 cups water, plus 30ml/2 tbsp extra

150g/5oz/1 cup fresh podded or frozen peas

50g/2oz/¼ cup 0% fat Greek (US strained plain) yogurt

15g/½oz/handful mixed fresh herbs, to include parsley, chives and/or mint

Juice of ½ lemon

Salt and cayenne pepper

To finish
15ml/1 tbsp olive oil
Few extra fresh herb leaves, optional

Energy 138kcal/581kJ; Protein 9.5g; Carbohydrate 17.6g, of which sugars 2.2g; Fat 3.9g, of which saturates 0.7g; Cholesterol 0mg; Calcium 53mg; Fibre 5.6g; Sodium 14mg.

Mung bean hummus with coriander

SERVES 4

Makes 450g/1lb/2 cups
Prep 20 minutes
Soak overnight
Cook 30 minutes

100g/3¾oz/½ cup dried
mung beans, soaked
overnight in cold water

1 litre/1¾ pints/4 cups water,
plus 30ml/2 tbsp extra

1 tomato, quartered,
deseeded and diced

1 orange, peeled, cut into
segments and diced

Seeds from ¼ pomegranate

2.5ml/½ tsp nigella seeds

15ml/1 tbsp olive oil

Salt and cayenne pepper

10g/¼oz/small handful fresh
coriander (cilantro)

15ml/1 tbsp tahini

Juice of ½ lemon

Unlike dried soaked chickpeas that can take anything up to 75 minutes to cook, soaked mung beans cook in around 30 minutes so are a much quicker option. Mixed with tangy herbs and topped with orange and pomegranate, this fresh fruity hummus makes for a very healthy snack or light lunch.

1 Drain the soaked beans and add to a pan with the water, bring to the boil and skim off any scum with a spoon. Half cover with a lid and simmer for about 30 minutes or until tender.

2 Drain the beans into a colander, cover with a clean dish towel and leave for 15–30 minutes to cool.

3 Add the tomato, orange and pomegranate seeds to a bowl. Stir in the nigella seeds, olive oil and a little salt and cayenne pepper and mix together, then spoon half this mix into the bowl of a food processor.

4 Finely chop about 15ml/1 tbsp of the fresh coriander and stir into the remaining tomato mix in the bowl with 30ml/2 tbsp of the cooked beans. Add the rest of the coriander, torn into pieces, and the rest of the beans to the bowl of the food processor with a little extra seasoning. Then add the tahini and lemon juice and blitz until smooth and speckled green.

5 Taste and adjust the seasoning and add the extra water if needed. Blitz again briefly.

6 Spoon into a bowl, swirl with the back of a spoon then sprinkle over the tomato mix topping. Serve with warmed flatbreads.

Energy 133kcal/559kJ; Protein 8g; Carbohydrate 14.8g, of which sugars 3.6g; Fat 5g, of which saturates 0.7g; Cholesterol 0mg; Calcium 27mg; Fibre 1g; Sodium 7mg.

HUMMUS SNACKS

Hummus is so much more than just a dip –
try this protein-packed, low-fat and low-carb
spread over wraps, add it to sandwiches,
even use it in place of tomato purée in a
pitta bread pizza or layered up in fashionable
mason jars for an easy-to-grab lunch to go.
Double the quantities if serving 4.

Hummus with spice-crusted cauliflower

SERVES 2

**Prep 10 minutes
Cook 4–6 minutes**

15ml/1 tbsp olive oil

½ cauliflower, cut into
bitesize florets (175g/6oz of
prepared florets)

1.5ml/¼ tsp turmeric

1.5ml/¼ tsp cumin seeds,
roughly crushed

2.5ml/½ tsp coriander seeds,
roughly crushed

25g/1oz/1 cup shredded kale

15g/½oz/⅛ cup unblanched
almonds, roughly chopped

200g/7oz/scant 1 cup
hummus, see page 36 or
hummus of choice

20ml/4 tsp chermoula sauce,
optional, see page 30

Cauliflower has come back into vogue and here it is quickly stir-fried with spices, kale and nuts to make a crunchy topping for creamy smooth hummus. This delicious snack takes no longer to do than making a sandwich.

1 Heat the oil in a frying pan, add the cauliflower then sprinkle with the spices and cook for 2–3 minutes, stirring, until just beginning to turn golden around the edges.

2 Add the kale and nuts to the pan and cook for 2–3 minutes more until the kale has softened and the nuts are browned.

3 Spoon the hummus over two serving plates then swirl in an even layer using the back of a spoon. Spoon the cauliflower mixture into the centre and serve immediately, drizzled with the chermoula sauce, if liked.

HEALTH NOTE Cauliflower contains sulforaphane, thought by some researchers to help slow the growth of some cancers, plus a range of vitamins, minerals, antioxidants and phytonutrients. It is also low in calories so is good news if you are watching your weight.

Energy 316kcal/1316kJ; Protein 12.8g; Carbohydrate 14.9g, of which sugars 4.6g; Fat 23.3g, of which saturates 2.9g; Cholesterol 0mg; Calcium 94mg; Fibre 5.8g; Sodium 685mg.

Kale and hummus bruschetta

Rather than butter or mayo, hummus makes a much healthier protein-based spread for an open sandwich or Italian bruschetta-style snack. Top with crispy kale and health-boosting nuts and seeds, and this really becomes a sandwich with a difference.

1 Heat the oil in a frying pan, add the garlic, pecan nuts and seeds and fry, stirring, over a gentle heat for a minute or two until just beginning to brown. Add the kale and stir-fry for 3 minutes until the kale is crispy and the nuts and seeds lightly browned.

2 Take the pan off the heat, toast the bread then spread with the hummus. Cut each slice in half, and arrange on serving plates. Sprinkle the kale, nuts and seeds on top, drizzle with the pomegranate molasses and balsamic vinegar, sprinkle with a few salt flakes, if using, and serve immediately.

HEALTH NOTE Packed with vitamins and minerals, pecan nuts are a high quality source of protein. They do contain fat, but the bulk of it is in the form of 60% monounsaturated and 30% polyunsaturated fats, so is heart-healthy.

SERVES 2

Prep 10 minutes
Cook 5 minutes

15ml/1 tbsp olive oil

1 garlic clove, finely chopped

20g/¾oz/generous ⅛ cup pecan nuts, halved

15ml/1 tbsp pumpkin seeds

15ml/1 tbsp sunflower seeds

40g/1½oz/1½ cups shredded kale

2 slices sourdough bread

100g/3¾oz/scant ½ cup hummus, see page 36 or hummus of choice

5ml/1 tsp pomegranate molasses

5ml/1 tsp balsamic vinegar

Few salt flakes, optional

Energy 437kcal/1825kJ; Protein 13g; Carbohydrate 35.6g, of which sugars 2.8g; Fat 27.9g, of which saturates 3.2g; Cholesterol 0mg; Calcium 124mg; Fibre 5.3g; Sodium 614mg.

Layered hummus salad

SERVES 2

Prep 20 minutes

½ x 400g/14oz can green lentils, drained, rinsed with cold water and drained again

20ml/4 tsp olive oil

10ml/2 tsp red wine vinegar

2.5ml/½ tsp tomato purée (paste)

Large pinch ground cumin

Salt and cayenne pepper

75g/3oz/1 small trimmed beetroot (beet), scrubbed and coarsely grated

1 tomato, diced

½ Little Gem (Bibb) lettuce, shredded

75g/3oz/1 small carrot, scrubbed and coarsely grated

5cm/2in piece cucumber, cut into small dice

½ yellow (bell) pepper, deseeded and diced

200g/7oz/scant 1 cup hummus, see page 36 or hummus of choice

10ml/2 tsp pumpkin seeds

10ml/2 tsp sunflower seeds

Trying to make a healthy lunch to take to work while juggling life can seem impossible, so why not make up this healthy super-colourful salad in two mason or large screw-topped jars the night before, then chill in the refrigerator for an easy lunch to just add to your bag the next day.

1 Spoon the lentils into the base of two 450–600ml/¾–1 pint glass jars. Fork the oil, vinegar, tomato purée and cumin together in a bowl then season with salt and cayenne pepper. Spoon over the lentils.

2 Divide the grated beetroot between the two jars then top with the tomato and then the lettuce. Cover with the carrot then add the cucumber and yellow pepper.

3 Spoon the hummus over the top of each jar, sprinkle with the seeds then screw on the lid. Chill until ready to serve.

HEALTH NOTE We should all be eating at least 5 portions of vegetables and fruit a day, yet how many of us actually manage that? This rainbow-coloured jar contains 3 out of the 5.

Energy 359kcal/1499kJ; Protein 15.1g; Carbohydrate 32.6g, of which sugars 11.6g; Fat 19.6g, of which saturates 2.6g; Cholesterol 0mg; Calcium 86mg; Fibre 10.1g; Sodium 709mg.

Lunchbox hummus special

If you are fed up with the same old dull sandwiches in your lunchbox then ring the changes with this healthy meat-free and dairy-free option.

1 Add the oil, lemon juice and tahini to a bowl then add the chia, sumac and sesame seeds and a little salt and cayenne pepper and fork together to make a dressing.

2 Stir the carrot, cabbage and kale into the dressing.

3 Cut the rolls in half, spoon the hummus over the bottom half of each roll then top with the salad and the roll lid. Wrap in baking parchment and pack into a lunchbox with a piece of fresh fruit and some cucumber sticks.

HEALTH NOTE Chickpeas and fresh vegetables are all rich in complex carbs and fibre; as these are broken down by the body slowly they leave you feeling fuller for longer and help to avoid the mood swings you get after munching on sugary snacks.
COOK'S TIP Sumac are tiny purple-coloured seeds popular in Middle Eastern cooking for their delicate lemony taste.

SERVES 2

Prep 10 minutes

15ml/1 tbsp olive oil

5ml/1 tsp lemon juice

5ml/1 tsp tahini

5ml/1 tsp chia seeds

1.5ml/¼ tsp sumac seeds

5ml/1 tsp sesame seeds

Salt and cayenne pepper

50g/2oz/1 small carrot, coarsely grated

50g/2oz red cabbage, finely shredded

15g/½oz/½ cup finely shredded spinach or kale

2 seeded wholemeal (whole-wheat) soft rolls

110g/4oz/generous ½ cup hummus, see page 36 or hummus of choice

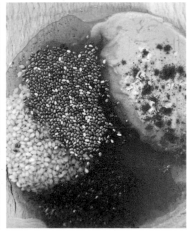

Energy 314kcal/1315kJ; Protein 10.8g; Carbohydrate 31.6g, of which sugars 5.1g; Fat 16.9g, of which saturates 2.5g; Cholesterol 0mg; Calcium 115mg; Fibre 6.5g; Sodium 640mg.

Triple-decker hummus and beetroot

SERVES 2

Prep 15 minutes

6 slices bread, lightly toasted

200g/7oz/1 scant cup hummus, see page 36 or hummus of choice

1 Little Gem (Bibb) lettuce, shredded

15g/½oz/1 large handful watercress or rocket (arugula)

90g/3½oz/2 small cooked beetroot (beet) in natural juices, drained and thinly sliced

1 medium orange, peeled, cut into segments

30g/1oz feta cheese, drained, crumbled

30g/1oz drained dill cucumber or gherkin, thinly sliced

This meat-free version tastes every bit as good as the more traditional café favourite made with chicken, bacon and mayo, and is bursting with vitamins, minerals, protein and good carbs.

1 Arrange the toast in a single layer on a chopping board, spread all the pieces with hummus then top 2 of the slices with the lettuce and watercress or rocket.

2 Add a second slice of hummus toast to the lettuce and watercress toast. Arrange the beetroot and orange on top then sprinkle with the feta cheese and cover with the dill cucumber slices.

3 Add the remaining toast, hummus side downwards, and press the sandwich stacks together. Cut each stack in half and secure the pieces with cocktail sticks or toothpicks. Transfer to serving plates or wrap in clear film or plastic wrap and baking parchment if adding to a lunchbox.

HEALTH NOTE Peppery watercress leaves are rich in vitamin K needed for bone-building and strengthening, vitamin A for good eye health, and the antioxidants lutein and zeaxanthin.

COOK'S TIP This sandwich will only be as good as the bread that you use, so choose a wholemeal (whole-wheat) seedy bread or rustic-style bread for texture.

Energy 469kcal/1978kJ; Protein 19g; Carbohydrate 63g, of which sugars 15.2g; Fat 17.5g, of which saturates 4g; Cholesterol 11mg; Calcium 253mg; Fibre 8.3g; Sodium 1346mg.

Steak and hummus wrap

A café-style steak sandwich takes on a Middle Eastern vibe with paprika-fried sirloin steak slices wrapped in a warm tortilla, spread with aubergine hummus (page 42) or smoky corn hummus (page 76) – or bought plain hummus, if you don't have time to make your own. Top with some crunchy lettuce, spinach, fresh coriander and roasted peppers, roll up and tuck in.

1 Preheat a large non-stick frying pan. Rub the steak on each side with a little salt and paprika then the oil, add to the pan and cook for 2 minutes each side for rare to medium or 4–5 minutes each side for well done. Take out of the pan and leave to rest while preparing the rest of the wrap.

2 Warm each of the tortillas in the steak pan one at a time. Place each tortilla on a square of baking parchment. Spread half the hummus all over each tortilla then arrange the lettuce and spinach in a row down the centre of each. Top with the fresh coriander, red pepper strips and dill cucumber. Add a little pickled chilli, if using.

3 Cut the steak into thin slices then arrange on the tortilla fillings. Fold in the ends of the tortillas then roll up tightly to enclose the fillings, using the parchment to hold everything together. Cut both wraps in half and serve immediately with a pile of paper napkins.

HEALTH NOTE Red meat tends to get a bad press from the nutritionists, but mostly it is because we eat it too often and in too generous a portion size. It is a valuable source of iron and protein. Trim off the fat before cooking and aim for a 110g/4oz portion. COOK'S TIP We all tend to over-cater when cooking a summer barbecue so why not use up some of the leftovers next day. Barbecued chicken, lamb, even sausages would all taste great in place of the steak in the tortilla above.

SERVES 2

Prep 15 minutes
Cook 4–10 minutes

225g/8oz/1 sirloin steak, fat trimmed away

Pinch salt

Little sweet paprika

10ml/2 tsp olive oil

2 large soft flour tortillas

110g/4oz/½ cup hummus

½ Little Gem (Bibb) lettuce, cut into strips

15g/½oz/½ cup baby spinach leaves

4 stems fresh coriander (cilantro)

100g/3¾oz/2 roasted (bell) peppers from a jar of brine, drained and cut into strips

40g/1½oz/1 small dill cucumber, drained and cut into strips

Few sliced pickled chillies, drained, optional

Energy 441kcal/1854kJ; Protein 34.3g; Carbohydrate 43.5g, of which sugars 5.2g; Fat 15.6g, of which saturates 3.4g; Cholesterol 65mg; Calcium 106mg; Fibre 4.9g; Sodium 645mg.

Baked sweet potato with hummus

SERVES 2

**Prep 10 minutes
Cook 45–60 minutes**

2 x 350g/12oz sweet
potatoes, scrubbed

2 tomatoes, diced

5cm/2in piece cucumber,
deseeded and diced

¼ red onion, finely chopped
or 1 spring onion (scallion)

½ yellow (bell) pepper,
cored, deseeded and diced

30ml/2 tbsp fresh chopped
parsley

15ml/1 tbsp olive oil

Juice of ½ lemon

110g/4oz/½ cup hummus,
see page 36 or hummus
of choice

A baked potato makes an easy hot lunch, but ring the changes by baking a sweet potato and topping with protein-rich but low-fat hummus instead of butter or cream cheese.

1 Preheat the oven to 200°C/400°F/Gas 6. Prick each potato several times with a fork then put on to a baking sheet and bake in the oven for 45–60 minutes or until soft.

2 Meanwhile mix the tomatoes, cucumber, onion and yellow pepper together in a bowl. Stir in the parsley, oil and lemon and set aside.

3 When the potatoes are cooked, make a slit along the length of each one, open out slightly and put on to 2 serving plates. Spoon the hummus into the centre of each one then top with the salad and serve.

HEALTH NOTE Sweet potatoes with their bright orange flesh are an excellent source of beta-carotene, converted by the body into vitamin A plus vitamin C, both powerful antioxidants which may help to protect against cancer.

Energy 494kcal/2090kJ; Protein 9.7g; Carbohydrate 88.1g, of which sugars 27.9g; Fat 14g, of which saturates 2.2g; Cholesterol 0mg; Calcium 118mg; Fibre 15.6g; Sodium 518mg.

Hummus and feta 'pizzas'

We all need a standby lunch every now and again. You will of course have your tub of hummus ready in the refrigerator. Feta keeps for months in the refrigerator, so too does a jar of sun-dried tomatoes, jar of roasted red peppers and a tube of tomato purée. Frozen pitta breads can be defrosted under a low grill so the only ingredient you may not have is some rocket or other green leaves, which can easily be left out.

1 Preheat the grill or broiler. Add the tomato, sun-dried tomatoes, red pepper and red onion to a bowl and mix together with a little oregano and salt and cayenne pepper.

2 Cook the pitta breads under the grill for a minute or two on each side until hot and puffy. Spread with the tomato purée then the hummus. Spoon over the tomato and pepper mixture then sprinkle with the feta cheese.

3 Grill for 2–3 minutes until the topping is hot and the feta is tinged golden brown. Drizzle with a little olive oil, if using. Transfer the pizzas to a board and scatter with rocket leaves. Serve immediately.

HEALTH NOTE Roasted red peppers are found in supermarkets in jars: choose those that are preserved in water or vinegar; they are much lower in calories than those preserved in oil at around 40 calories and between 1–1.7g salt per 100g. Keep in the refrigerator once opened.

SERVES 2

Prep 10 minutes
Cook 6 minutes

1 tomato, diced

15g/½oz drained sun-dried tomatoes in oil, roughly chopped

40g/1½oz/1 drained roasted red (bell) pepper from a jar, (in light brine), roughly chopped

¼ small red onion, thinly sliced

Pinch dried oregano

Salt and cayenne pepper

2 pitta breads

10ml/2 tsp tomato purée (paste)

110g/4oz/ ½ cup hummus, see page 36

40g/1½oz feta cheese, drained and crumbled

10ml/2 tsp olive oil, optional

15g/½oz/handful rocket (arugula) leaves

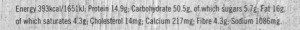

Energy 393kcal/1651kJ; Protein 14.9g; Carbohydrate 50.5g, of which sugars 5.7g; Fat 16g, of which saturates 4.3g; Cholesterol 14mg; Calcium 217mg; Fibre 4.3g; Sodium 1086mg.

Egg on flatbread toast Middle Eastern-style

This classic snack gets a hummus makeover for a quick and easy lunch, or even supper. It makes a welcome change from a frozen pizza and takes about the same time to bake.

1 Preheat the oven to 190°C/375°F/Gas 5. Put the flatbreads on to a large baking sheet then spread the hummus over the top of each.

2 Heat the butter in a frying pan, add the mushrooms and cook for 2–3 minutes until just beginning to colour. Add the garlic and spinach and cook for 2 minutes until just wilted. Season with salt and cayenne pepper and spoon over the flatbreads.

3 Make a dip in the centre of the vegetables on each flatbread then break an egg into the dip. Bake for 10–12 minutes until the egg whites are set, the yolks still soft and the flatbreads hot.

4 Transfer to serving plates. Mix the harissa and oil together, drizzle over the eggs and serve immediately.

COOK'S TIP If you don't have any harissa then add a little sweet chilli sauce or a little finely chopped red or green chilli to taste.

SERVES 2

**Prep 10 minutes
Cook 14–17 minutes**

2 x 18cm/7in flame-baked chapatis or a 180g/6oz pack of similar sized flatbreads, see also page 138

150g/5oz/¾ cup hummus, see page 36 or hummus of choice

25g/1oz butter

175g/6oz closed cup mushrooms, sliced

1 garlic clove, finely chopped

50g/2oz/2 cups baby spinach

Salt and cayenne pepper

2 eggs

5ml/1 tsp harissa paste

10ml/2 tsp olive oil

Energy 550kcal/2303kJ; Protein 22.1g; Carbohydrate 48.9g, of which sugars 3.5g; Fat 31g, of which saturates 10.2g; Cholesterol 258mg; Calcium 169mg; Fibre 4.4g; Sodium 810mg.

HUMMUS MEALS

Incorporate hummus into your main meal by spreading it over the serving plate as an alternative to mashed potato, rice or pasta, then top with meatballs, slow-cooked tagines or casseroles, or barbecued meaty skewers. Much more than a dip, hummus can be used in all kinds of ways in other dishes.

Hummus with herby meatballs

SERVES 4

**Prep 15 minutes
Cook 22 minutes**

15ml/1 tbsp olive oil
24 beef meatballs (2 x 350g/
12oz packs if ready-made)
2 garlic cloves, finely chopped
5ml/1 tsp coriander seeds,
roughly crushed
1 bunch spring onions
(scallions), thinly sliced, white
and green tops kept separate
300ml/½ pint/1¼ cups
chicken stock
150g/5oz/generous 1 cup
frozen edamame beans or
broad (fava) beans
110g/4oz/¾ cup frozen peas
10ml/2 tsp cornflour
(cornstarch)
Juice of ½ lemon
Salt and cayenne pepper
45ml/3 tbsp chopped fresh dill
45ml/3 tbsp chopped fresh
flat leaf parsley
450g/1lb/2 cups hummus, see
page 36 or hummus of choice

We are perhaps more used to serving meatballs with pasta or rice, but hummus makes a great alternative. Spread the hummus over the plate with a spoon, shaping the edges to make a rim to hold the lovely herby juices, then dive in with a spoon for a taste sensation.

1 Heat the oil in a large frying pan, add the meatballs and fry for 5 minutes over a medium heat, turning frequently until evenly browned.

2 Add the garlic, coriander seeds and white parts of the onions and fry for 2 minutes until the onion has just softened.

3 Pour in the stock then cover and simmer for 10 minutes until the meatballs are almost cooked through. Add the frozen vegetables and cook for 3 minutes.

4 Mix the cornflour to a paste with the lemon juice, stir into the sauce with a little salt and cayenne pepper then sprinkle over the green tops of the spring onions. Cook, stirring for 2 minutes until the sauce has thickened and the meatballs are cooked through, then mix in the chopped herbs.

5 Spread the hummus over serving plates or shallow bowls then top with the meatballs, vegetables and sauce and serve immediately.

HEALTH NOTE Frozen vegetables are harvested and frozen within hours for maximum nutrition levels. Edamame beans look just like broad beans but are much higher in protein and make a great addition to soups and salads or can be mixed into hummus itself. Frozen peas contain vitamin B, vitamin C, phosphorus and fibre. As the vegetables are frozen there is no waste, just take out what you need, when you need them, and add straight to the pan.
COOK'S TIP If you don't have any dill then use chopped fresh mint instead.

Energy 667kcal/2774kJ; Protein 45.6g; Carbohydrate 21.2g, of which sugars 3.8g; Fat 45g, of which saturates 14g; Cholesterol 101mg; Calcium 84mg; Fibre 8.1g; Sodium 892mg.

Musabaha

Each country or region has its own comfort food, and in the eastern Mediterranean and Middle East it is musabaha or masabacha. Hummus is topped with slow-cooked and gently spiced chickpeas, a spoonful of tahini and an egg that has been hard-boiled for 8 hours (although a more usual 8-minute egg works just fine).

1 Drain the soaked chickpeas into a colander then tip into a pan. Pour over the water and stir in the bicarbonate of soda and crushed seeds. Bring the water to the boil then skim off the scum with a spoon, half cover with a lid and simmer for 40–60 minutes or until the chickpeas are tender and still hold their shape.

2 When the chickpeas are almost ready, add the eggs to a pan of cold water, bring the water to the boil and then hard-boil for 8 minutes. Drain, rinse with cold water, crack the shells then peel and set aside.

3 Drain the cooked chickpeas into a colander set over a bowl – keep back a little of the cooking water. Heat the oil in a large frying pan, add the garlic and chilli and cook for 2 minutes over a medium heat to release the flavours. Add the warm chickpeas and cook for 2–3 minutes, stirring until coated in the seeds and chilli.

4 Stir in the tahini, some of the reserved cooking liquid to moisten and salt to taste, and cook for a minute or two.

5 Spread the hummus over serving plates and spoon the chickpeas over the top. Cut the eggs into wedges, add to the chickpeas and sprinkle with paprika and parsley. Serve immediately with lemon wedges to squeeze over, and a small bottle of olive oil so diners can add extra, if liked.

SERVES 4

Prep 20 minutes
Cook 45–65 minutes

200g/7oz/1 cup dried chickpeas, soaked overnight in cold water

2 litres/3½ pints/8 cups water

2.5ml/½ tsp bicarbonate of soda (baking soda)

5ml/1 tsp cumin seeds, roughly crushed

5ml/1 tsp coriander seeds, roughly crushed

4 eggs

45ml/3 tbsp olive oil

3 garlic cloves, sliced

1–2 green chillies, deseeded and finely chopped, to taste

30ml/2 tbsp tahini

Salt

450g/1lb/2 cups hummus, see page 36

10ml/2 tsp sweet paprika

Little roughly chopped fresh flat leaf parsley, to garnish

Lemon wedges and extra olive oil, to serve

Energy 582kcal/2434kJ; Protein 28.5g; Carbohydrate 38.7g, of which sugars 3.5g; Fat 35.9g, of which saturates 5.6g; Cholesterol 231mg; Calcium 165mg; Fibre 10.7g; Sodium 858mg.

Couscous with aubergine and hummus

SERVES 4

Prep 25 minutes
Cook 30 minutes

2 x 300g/11oz aubergines (eggplants)

60ml/4 tbsp olive oil

10ml/2 tsp harissa paste

2 garlic cloves, finely chopped

Salt and cayenne pepper

200g/7oz/1 generous cup couscous

350ml/12fl oz/1½ cups boiling water

Grated zest and juice of ½ lemon

3 spring onions (scallions), finely chopped

2 tomatoes, diced

100g/3¾oz/2 roasted red (bell) peppers from a jar of light brine, drained and diced

45ml/3 tbsp fresh chopped mint

45ml/3 tbsp fresh chopped parsley

200g/7oz/1 scant cup hummus, see page 36 or hummus of choice

30g/1oz/1 handful rocket (arugula) leaves

Little drizzle of extra olive oil, optional

Rather than a base, hummus is served here as a tasty protein-boosting topping to a garlicky spiced and roasted aubergine. Choose from a traditional hummus, see page 36, or a flavoured one, perhaps with smoky corn (page 76) or spinach (page 44).

1 Preheat the oven to 200°C/400°F/Gas 6. Cut each aubergine in half lengthways, put into a roasting pan and make criss-cross cuts over the top. Mix half the oil and half the harissa with all of the garlic, then spread over the aubergine. Sprinkle with a little salt and cayenne pepper and roast for 30 minutes or until they are tender.

2 Meanwhile, add the couscous to a large bowl, pour over the boiling water then cover with a plate. Leave to soak for 5 minutes.

3 To make a dressing, mix together the remaining olive oil and harissa, lemon zest and juice then season with salt and cayenne pepper.

4 Fluff the couscous up with a fork then stir in the dressing. Mix in the onions, tomatoes, peppers and herbs then re-cover with the plate and set aside.

5 When the aubergines are ready, spoon the couscous over serving plates, top each with a roasted aubergine half then a generous spoonful of hummus. Garnish with rocket leaves and drizzle with extra olive oil if liked.

COOK'S TIP If you are not a fan of aubergine then substitute with thick slices of cauliflower, spread with the harissa and garlic mix and roast for 15 minutes.

Energy 350kcal/1460kJ; Protein 9.1g; Carbohydrate 38.3g, of which sugars 7.4g; Fat 18.8g, of which saturates 2.6g; Cholesterol 0mg; Calcium 83mg; Fibre 7.8g; Sodium 364mg.

Hummus with honey-glazed chicken skewers

With hot chicken skewers cooked over charcoal, and served on lovely cool hummus, this light summery supper will bring back holiday memories from Turkey and the Middle East. If the weather is against you, all is not lost, cook the skewers under the grill or broiler or use a ridged frying pan if you have one.

1 Add the oil, orange juice, honey, paprika and oregano to a bowl with a little salt and cayenne pepper. Fork together then add the chicken and mix together. Cover the bowl with clear film or plastic wrap and marinade in the refrigerator for 30 minutes, or longer if there is time.

2 Stir the chicken once more then thread on to 8 metal skewers and either cook on a barbecue, under a preheated grill, or on a griddle pan, for about 10–12 minutes, turning once or twice until the chicken is a deep brown and cooked right through with no pink juices.

3 Spread the hummus over the serving plates with the back of a spoon. Add 2 chicken skewers, a spoonful of yogurt, a sprinkling of paprika, some chopped herbs and pomegranate seeds, if using, and serve immediately.

HEALTH NOTE Chicken is rich in protein which is key to create new cells, maintain and repair existing cells and to produce enzymes which aid digestion, metabolism and storage of fats. With just 1g of saturated fat and 4g of total fat per 100g/3¾oz cooked, boneless, skinless chicken breast is a low-fat food too.
COOK'S TIP If you don't have any metal skewers then use wooden ones, but make sure to soak in cold water while the chicken marinades to lessen the chances of them burning during cooking.

SERVES 4

Prep 15 minutes
Marinade 30 minutes
Cook 10–12 minutes

30ml/2 tbsp olive oil
60ml/4 tbsp/¼ cup freshly squeezed orange juice
10ml/2 tsp clear honey
5ml/1 tsp sweet or mild paprika, plus extra to garnish
5ml/1 tsp dried oregano
Salt and cayenne pepper
500g/1lb 2oz boneless, skinless chicken breasts, cut into cubes
450g/1lb/2 cups hummus, see page 36 or hummus of choice
60ml/4 tbsp/¼ cup Greek (US strained plain) 0% fat yogurt
Little roughly chopped fresh mint or flat leaf parsley
Few pomegranate seeds, optional

Energy 413kcal/1731kJ; Protein 39.5g; Carbohydrate 17.5g, of which sugars 6.6g; Fat 21.1g, of which saturates 2.9g; Cholesterol 88mg; Calcium 78mg; Fibre 3.6g; Sodium 841mg.

Hummus with spiced beef and cherries

SERVES 4

Prep 15 minutes
Cook 20 minutes

15ml/1 tbsp olive oil

500g/1lb 2oz lean minced (ground) beef

1 onion, chopped

2 garlic cloves, finely chopped

2.5ml/½ tsp ground cinnamon

10ml/2 tsp sweet paprika

15ml/1 tbsp za'atar spice mix, see page 29

5 allspice berries, crushed or 1.5ml/¼ tsp ground

25g/1oz/2 tbsp sultanas (golden raisins)

150ml/¼ pint/⅔ cup beef stock

Salt and cayenne pepper

30g/1oz/scant ¼ cup dried cherries

30ml/2 tbsp boiling water

450g/1lb/2 cups hummus, see page 36 or hummus of choice

Little extra olive oil, optional

110g/4oz/scant ½ cup Greek (US strained plain) 0% fat yogurt

40g/1½oz/handful fresh flat leaf parsley, roughly chopped

Little tarator sauce, see page 31, optional

We often add a pack of mince or ground meat to our supermarket trolley, but it can be used for so much more than just spaghetti bolognese or shepherd's pie. This easy supper is made by frying minced beef – but you might also like to try minced lamb – with garlic, spices and just a small amount of stock. Serve on the hummus base with dried cherries for a sweet and sour hit, fresh-tasting parsley and a spoonful of cooling yogurt.

1 Heat the oil in a frying pan with a lid, add the beef and fry over a medium heat for 5 minutes, stirring until lightly browned. Add the onion and garlic and fry for 5 more minutes, stirring until the onion is golden.

2 Mix in the spices, sultanas and stock. Season with salt and cayenne pepper then cover the pan and fry for 10 minutes, stirring from time to time. Meanwhile add the dried cherries to a bowl and soak in the boiling water. Stir the beef once more then sprinkle the cherries over the top.

3 Spoon the hummus on to serving plates, then spread over the plates with the back of a spoon. Top with the beef mix, drizzle with a little extra olive oil, if liked, then add a large spoonful of yogurt to each and sprinkle with parsley. Add a little tarator sauce, if using, and serve immediately.

HEALTH NOTE Dried fruit adds a concentrated nutrient boost to sweet and savoury recipes. Sultanas or dried golden raisins add B vitamins plus natural sugars to boost energy. Tart-tasting dried cherries add more of a sweet and sour hit, and they are a good source of copper – an essential mineral for collagen production and to help cells produce energy, plus vitamins A and C. There is anecdotal evidence that if you are a gout sufferer, you can reduce outbreaks if you eat a handful of dried cherries everyday.

COOK'S TIP Dried cranberries or a sprinkling of fresh, stoned or pitted and quartered cherries can be used instead of the dried cherries.

Energy 529kcal/2212kJ; Protein 38.9g; Carbohydrate 28.4g, of which sugars 15.5g; Fat 29.7g, of which saturates 7.5g; Cholesterol 70mg; Calcium 145mg; Fibre 5.1g; Sodium 894mg.

Chermoula lamb with griddled courgettes and hummus

SERVES 4

Chermoula is a quick and easy-to-make raw herb and garlic sauce that adds a taste sensation to salad dressings, marinades or simply spooned or swirled into hummus. It pairs perfectly with lamb on a hummus base.

1 First make the chermoula sauce by adding the garlic, herbs and chilli to the bowl of a food processor. Blitz until finely chopped then add the cumin seeds, olive oil and lemon juice. Season with salt and cayenne pepper and mix together briefly.

2 Spoon half the chermoula sauce into a plastic container then stir in the yogurt and diced lamb. Cover with the lid and chill for 4 hours in the refrigerator or longer if time.

3 Arrange the courgette slices over a large plate and brush with some of the remaining chermoula sauce. Cover with clear film or plastic wrap and chill until ready to cook.

4 When ready to serve, preheat the grill or broiler, a ridged frying pan or the barbecue. Lift the lamb pieces out of the yogurt and thread on to 8 small metal skewers. Cook the courgette first, in two batches, for 2 minutes each side until just softened but still bright green and keep hot. Cook the lamb skewers for 10–15 minutes, turning until browned and crusty looking and the meat is still slightly pink in the centre.

5 Spoon the hummus on to serving plates and spread into an even layer. Arrange the courgette slices in the centre, then remove the lamb from the skewers and arrange on top. Serve with any remaining chermoula sauce drizzled over and garnish with some torn herb leaves.

Prep 30 minutes
Marinade 4 hours
Cook 18–23 minutes

100g/3¾oz/scant ½ cup Greek (US strained plain) 0% fat yogurt

600g/1lb 6oz/6 small boneless lamb leg steaks, cut into chunks

2 courgettes (zucchini), total weight 450g/1lb, cut into thin diagonal slices

450g/1lb/2 cups hummus, see page 36 or hummus of choice

Little torn fresh coriander (cilantro) and parsley leaves

For the chermoula sauce – makes 100g/3¾oz/½ cup

2 garlic cloves, sliced

25g/1oz/1 large handful of mixed fresh coriander (cilantro) and flat leaf parsley

1 large red chilli, halved, deseeded and chopped

5ml/1 tsp cumin seeds, roughly crushed

30ml/2 tbsp olive oil

Juice of 1 lemon

Salt and cayenne pepper

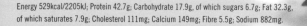

Energy 529kcal/2205kJ; Protein 42.7g; Carbohydrate 17.9g, of which sugars 6.7g; Fat 32.3g, of which saturates 7.9g; Cholesterol 111mg; Calcium 149mg; Fibre 5.5g; Sodium 882mg.

Hummus, spinach and sweet potato borek

SERVES 6

**Prep 20 minutes
Cook 38–40 minutes**

500g/1lb 2oz/2 small sweet potatoes, peeled and cut into cubes

1 red onion, halved and thinly sliced

30ml/2 tbsp olive oil

1.5ml/¼ tsp hot smoked paprika or chilli powder

1.5ml/¼ tsp cumin seeds, roughly crushed

Salt

110g/4oz/4 cups baby spinach

40g/1½oz butter, plus extra for greasing

270g/10oz pack of 6 sheets of chilled or frozen filo pastry, defrosted

225g/8oz/1 cup hummus, see page 36, or hummus of choice

100g/3¾oz/½ cup cooked lentils from a 400g/14oz can, drained

100g/3¾oz/½ pack feta cheese, drained

5ml/1 tsp sesame seeds

5ml/1 tsp nigella seeds, optional

These filo pastries are sold on every street corner in Turkey and Syria; they can be tiny bitesize triangles, larger cigar shapes, or even bigger. These individual pies are made with a base of hummus topped with roasted sweet potato, red onion, spinach and feta. Choose plain hummus or if you have some, a flavoured hummus such as chargrilled aubergine (page 42) or red pepper (page 54).

1 Preheat the oven to 200°C/400°F/Gas 6. Add the sweet potatoes and onion to a roasting pan, drizzle with the oil and sprinkle with the paprika or chilli powder, cumin seeds and a little salt. Roast for 20 minutes, turning the vegetables after 10 minutes.

2 Add the spinach to the roasting pan, turn in the pan juices then roast for 3–5 minutes until the leaves have just wilted. Butter 6 x 12cm/4½in loose-bottomed tart tins or pie pans.

3 Melt the butter in a small pan and put to one side. Unfold the pastry sheets and put one of the sheets in front of you, then cut into 2 squares. Brush each with a little of the melted butter then drape one of the pieces into a tart tin or pie pan. Add the second piece of pastry at a slight angle to the first one.

4 Spoon one-sixth of the hummus into the base of the pastry-lined tin, add one sixth of the lentils then one-sixth of the roasted vegetables. Sprinkle with a little crumbled feta cheese then fold the pastry over the filling. Repeat to make 6 boreks.

5 Brush the tops of the boreks with the remaining butter and sprinkle with the seeds. Bake for about 15 minutes until the tops are golden brown and the base of the pastries are crisp and golden. Leave to cool for 10 minutes then loosen and take out of the tins. Serve warm or cold with salad.

Energy 410kcal/1720kJ; Protein 11.8g; Carbohydrate 52g, of which sugars 7.3g; Fat 18.7g, of which saturates 7.2g; Cholesterol 26mg; Calcium 191mg; Fibre 6.9g; Sodium 565mg.

Roast vegetable and hummus tart

You don't need loads of effort to make this fabulous tart, simply unroll a pack of ready-rolled puff pastry, mark with a knife and bake. What could be easier!

1 Preheat the oven to 200°C/400°F/Gas 6. Add the courgette, orange and red pepper and fennel to a roasting pan, drizzle with the oil and sprinkle with the rosemary and a little salt. Roast for 20 minutes.

2 Meanwhile, unroll the puff pastry sheet and put on to a lightly oiled baking sheet. Take a very thin sliver of pastry off each side to aid rising. Mark a line 2.5cm/1in in from the outer edge to make a smaller rectangle then prick inside this smaller rectangle with a fork. Brush the pastry lightly with beaten egg then bake for 15 minutes.

3 Turn the vegetables and add the cherry tomatoes to the roasting pan. Press the inner rectangle of pastry down to make a tart case and put both the vegetables and the pastry back in the oven for 10 minutes.

4 Transfer the hot tart case to a chopping board. Spread the hummus over the inner rectangle of pastry. Peel away the pepper skins, if preferred, then cut into bitesize pieces. Arrange all the roasted vegetables over the hummus. Sprinkle with any reserved fennel fronds and chopped parsley. Serve cut into pieces with salad.

COOK'S TIP You might also like to make some tarator (page 31) or chermoula sauce (page 30) and drizzle a little over the tart.

SERVES 6

**Prep 20 minutes
Cook 30 minutes**

200g/7oz/1 courgette (zucchini), sliced

1 orange (bell) pepper, quartered, deseeded and cored

1 red (bell) pepper, quartered, deseeded and cored

110g/4oz/1 fennel bulb, cut into chunks and any green fronds reserved

30ml/2 tbsp olive oil

1 stem fresh rosemary, leaves torn from stem

Little coarse sea salt

320g/11½oz pack of 1 ready-rolled sheet of puff pastry

Little beaten egg for glazing

175g/6oz cherry tomatoes, halved

350g/12oz/1½ cups hummus, see page 36, or hummus of choice

Little chopped fresh parsley, to garnish

Energy 373kcal/1555kJ; Protein 9g; Carbohydrate 32.1g, of which sugars 7.2g; Fat 24g, of which saturates 7.5g; Cholesterol 30mg; Calcium 74mg; Fibre 4.5g; Sodium 564mg.

Sesame chicken with hummus and green vegetables

Super-tasty, this dish contains just about everything that you need to make up a healthy meal: a good mix of nutrient- and antioxidant-packed vegetables, high-protein chicken and chickpeas, good fats and good carbs.

1 Add the chicken to a plastic container or bowl, drizzle over 30ml/2 tbsp of the oil and lemon juice then add the garlic, crushed cumin and coriander seeds, sesame seeds and a little salt and cayenne pepper. Mix together. Cover with a lid and chill in the refrigerator for 30 minutes, longer if time, for the flavours to mingle together.

2 When ready to serve, heat a large nonstick frying pan, add the chicken and spread into a single layer. Cook for 10–12 minutes, turning once or twice until evenly browned and the chicken is cooked through with no hint of pink juices. Add the broccoli after 5 minutes. Scoop out of the pan and put aside in a bowl, keeping warm if possible.

3 Add a little extra oil if needed to the pan then add the asparagus and cook for 3 minutes, stirring until just softened. Add the tomatoes, and cook for 1–2 minutes until hot. Return the chicken to the pan to reheat if needed.

4 Spread the hummus over the serving plates. Top with the vegetables and chicken and serve immediately.

HEALTH NOTE The darker the colour of broccoli florets the higher the amounts of vitamin C and beta–carotene (which the body converts into vitamin A) they contain. Broccoli also contains beneficial indoles, and nitrogen compounds which may help to protect DNA from damage and so help to protect from cancer.

SERVES 4

Prep 20 minutes
Marinade 30 minutes
Cook 20–22 minutes

500g/1lb 2oz/4 small boneless, skinless chicken breasts, cut into long thin strips

45ml/3 tbsp olive oil

Juice of ½ lemon

2 garlic cloves, finely chopped

5ml/1 tsp cumin seeds, roughly crushed

5ml/1 tsp coriander seeds, roughly crushed

20ml/4 tsp sesame seeds

Salt and cayenne pepper

150g/5oz purple-sprouting broccoli, trimmed and cut into thin strips

200g/7oz/1 bunch asparagus, trimmed

175g/6oz cherry tomatoes, halved

450g/1lb/2 cups hummus, see page 36 or hummus of choice

Energy 481kcal/2009kJ; Protein 42.7g; Carbohydrate 16.4g, of which sugars 5.2g; Fat 27.6g, of which saturates 4g; Cholesterol 88mg; Calcium 179mg; Fibre 7.6g; Sodium 840mg.

BREADS FOR DIPPING

Nothing beats the smell of homemade bread as it bakes. Mixing and kneading the bread is therapeutic (and fun for kids to be involved with as well). Mix and leave the dough to rise while the chickpeas cook for hummus, then finish off later. Or if you don't have much time, the pan-fried flatbreads are made without yeast and don't need rising.

Ekmek

Many versions of flatbread can be found throughout the Mediterranean. This Turkish country bread is similar to Italian focaccia and is topped with sesame seeds but you can also try poppy seeds, nigella seeds or za'atar spice mix. Why not eat one or two of the breads and freeze the third well-wrapped in foil for another time; just warm it through in the oven before serving.

1 Add the flour, salt and yeast to the bowl of your electric mixer fitted with the dough hook, or into a large mixing bowl. Add the honey and half the olive oil then gradually mix in enough warm water to make a soft dough.

2 Knead for 5 minutes until the dough is very smooth and elastic either in the mixer or turned out on to a lightly floured work surface. Put the dough into a bowl, cover with oiled clear film or plastic wrap and leave in a warm place to rise for about 1 hour or until doubled in size.

3 Knock the dough back with your fist then scoop out of the bowl on to a lightly floured work surface. Cut into 3 even-sized pieces then knead each into a smooth ball. Roll out each piece to a rough-shaped round about 20cm/8in in diameter.

4 Transfer the breads to 2 or 3 lightly oiled baking sheets depending on their size. Cover loosely with oiled clear film and leave again in a warm place for 30 minutes until well risen. Meanwhile preheat the oven to 220°C/425°F/Gas 7.

5 Brush the breads lightly with the remaining oil. Make 4 cuts across each bread, then 4 more cuts at right angles to the first. Sprinkle with sesame seeds and bake for about 15 minutes or until golden brown and the breads sound hollow when tapped. Transfer to a wire rack to cool slightly then serve warm with hummus and salad.

MAKES 3

Prep 25 minutes
Rising 1½ hours
Cook 15 minutes

500g/1¼lb/scant 4½ cups strong white bread flour

5ml/1 tsp salt

10g/2½ tsp easy-blend (rapid-rise) dried yeast

15ml/1 tbsp clear honey

60ml/4 tbsp olive oil

300ml/½ pint/1¼ cups warm water

45ml/3 tbsp sesame seeds

Energy 813kcal/3428kJ; Protein 18.4g; Carbohydrate 135.7g, of which sugars 8.7g; Fat 25.5g, of which saturates 4g; Cholesterol 0mg; Calcium 334mg; Fibre 8.5g; Sodium 664mg.

Lavash

These large flatbreads are thinner and crisper than others and make great dippers for hummus. They are topped with millet, but sesame seeds or crushed cumin or coriander seeds could also be sprinkled over the top. They are best eaten warm from the oven, but leftovers can be frozen in a plastic container for another time.

1 Add the flour, salt, sugar and yeast to the bowl of your electric mixer fitted with a dough hook, or large mixing bowl. Add the olive oil and gradually mix in enough warm water to make a soft dough.

2 Knead for 5 minutes until the dough is smooth and elastic in the mixer or turn out on to a lightly floured surface. Put the dough into a bowl, cover with oiled clear film or plastic wrap and put in a warm place to rise for about 1 hour or until doubled in size. Preheat the oven to 220°C/425°F/Gas 7.

3 Knock the dough back with your fist then scoop out of the bowl on to a lightly floured work surface. Cut into 10 pieces and shape each into a ball. Roll out each piece of dough thinly on a lightly floured work surface into a rough-shaped round about 15–18cm/6–7in in diameter. Transfer to lightly floured baking sheets. Loosely cover with oiled clear film and leave to rise for 20–30 minutes until puffy.

4 Peel the clear film off the breads, brush the tops with the milk and sprinkle with the seeds. Bake for 5–7 minutes until lightly puffed and browned.

TO MAKE PITTA BREADS The lavash bread recipe can also be used to make pitta breads. Cut the risen dough into the same number of pieces but shape into smaller thicker ovals about the size of your hand. Bake on heated baking sheets for 5–10 minutes until lightly tinged brown.

MAKES 10

Prep 35 minutes
Rising 1½ hours
Cook 5–7 minutes

500g/1¼lb/scant 4½ cups strong white bread flour

5ml/1 tsp salt

5ml/1 tsp caster (superfine) sugar

10g/2½ tsp easy-blend (rapid-rise) dried yeast

30ml/2 tbsp olive oil

300ml/½ pint/1¼ cups warm water

30ml/2 tbsp milk, to glaze

30ml/2 tbsp millet seeds

Energy 210kcal/887kJ; Protein 5.3g; Carbohydrate 39.3g, of which sugars 1.2g; Fat 4.6g, of which saturates 0.7g; Cholesterol 0mg; Calcium 90mg; Fibre 2.4g; Sodium 199mg.

Bread sticks

There is something comforting about kneading and shaping bread. Encourage the kids to have a go, it really doesn't matter if the sticks are different thicknesses.

1 Add the flour, salt, sugar and yeast to the bowl of your electric mixer fitted with a dough hook, or into a large mixing bowl. Add the oil and gradually mix in enough warm water to make a soft dough.

2 Knead for 5 minutes until the dough is very smooth and elastic either in the mixer or turn out on to a lightly floured work surface. Put the dough into a bowl, cover with oiled clear film or plastic wrap and put in a warm place to rise for about 1 hour or until doubled in size.

3 Knock the dough back with your fist then scoop out of the bowl on to a lightly floured work surface. Knead well then cut into 4 pieces. Leave one of the pieces plain, knead the sesame seeds into the second piece of dough, the rosemary into the third, and the fennel seeds into the last piece.

4 Cut the plain dough into 8 then roll each piece into a rope about 25cm/10in long. Arrange slightly spaced apart on a lightly oiled baking sheet. Repeat with the other flavoured doughs to make 32 bread sticks in all.

5 Cover the bread sticks with lightly oiled clear film, and leave in a warm place for about 30 minutes until well risen. Preheat the oven to 220°C/425°F/Gas 7.

6 Remove the clear film, brush the breadsticks with a little beaten egg and sprinkle the plain sticks with a little salt, if liked. Bake for 6–8 minutes until golden. Loosen the bread sticks with a palette knife then slide the sticks on to a wire rack to cool.

MAKES ABOUT 32

Prep 35 minutes
Rising 1½ hours
Cook 6–8 minutes

500g/1¼lb/scant 4½ cups strong white bread flour

5ml/1 tsp salt

5ml/1 tsp caster (superfine) sugar

10g/2½ tsp easy-blend (rapid-rise) dried yeast

30ml/2 tbsp olive oil

300ml/½ pint/1¼ cups warm water

30ml/2 tbsp sesame seeds

15ml/1 tbsp fresh chopped rosemary leaves

10ml/2 tsp fennel seeds

Little beaten egg, to glaze

Few salt flakes, optional

Energy 66kcal/277kJ; Protein 1.7g; Carbohydrate 12.3g, of which sugars 0.4g; Fat 1.5g, of which saturates 0.2g; Cholesterol 0mg; Calcium 32mg; Fibre 0.7g; Sodium 62mg.

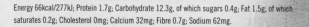

Speedy yeast-free flatbreads

MAKES 4

Prep 10 minutes
Rest 15 minutes
Cook 15 minutes

75g/3oz/⅔ cup self-raising
(self-rising) wholemeal
(whole-wheat) flour

75g/3oz/⅔ cup self-raising
(self-rising) white flour

Pinch salt

2.5ml/½ tsp cumin seeds,
roughly crushed

100–120ml/3½–4fl oz/
scant ½–½ cup cold water

15ml/1 tbsp sunflower oil

We have all had those moments when you reach into the bread bin to find it empty. These easy flatbreads are made with half wholemeal and half white self-raising flour and as the raising agent is already in the flour there is no need for yeast. You don't even need to turn the oven on; just cook each one in a large lightly oiled frying pan for a few minutes until air bubbles appear on the top and there are scorchmarks on the underside.

1 Add the flours, salt and cumin seeds to a mixing bowl. Gradually mix in just enough water to mix to a soft but not sticky dough. Lightly knead into a smooth ball then put back in the bowl and cover with a clean dish towel, and set aside for 15 minutes.

2 Cut the dough into 4 pieces and roll out each piece on a lightly floured surface to make a rough-shaped circle about 18cm/7in in diameter.

3 Preheat a dry non-stick frying pan, add the oil to a piece of folded kitchen paper then rub over the frying pan, add one of the breads and cook over a moderate heat for 2–3 minutes until brown scorchmarks appear on the base and bubbles are visible on the top. Turn the bread over and cook the second side for 1 minute.

4 Slide the flatbread out on to a clean dish towel and keep hot. Repeat until all 4 flatbreads have been cooked.

COOK'S TIP The flatbreads can seem a little firm when they are first cooked but wrapping in a clean dish towel not only keeps them hot but traps in the steam which softens the bread.

Energy 147kcal/621kJ; Protein 4.2g; Carbohydrate 26.6g, of which sugars 0.7g; Fat 3.4g, of which saturates 0.4g; Cholesterol 0mg; Calcium 34mg; Fibre 3g; Sodium 1mg.

Gluten-free za'atar flatbreads

Just because gluten is off the menu it doesn't mean that flatbreads are. These easy-to-make breads contain gram or chickpea flour and rice flour, which are gluten-free. As the dough doesn't contain yeast it only needs to be left to rest for 15 minutes before being quickly cooked in a frying pan.

1 Sift the gram flour into a bowl then mix in the rice flour, salt and xanthum gum if using. Stir in the spice mix. Add the butter then gradually mix in enough water to mix to a soft, slightly sticky dough. Cover the bowl with a dish towel and leave to stand for 15 minutes.

2 Scoop the soft dough out of the bowl, and cut into 12 pieces. Roll one of the pieces out between two pieces of clear film, plastic wrap or baking parchment to a rough-shaped oval about 10cm/5in long. Repeat and make a second one in the same way.

3 Heat a little oil in a large frying pan, peel off the clear film, wrap or parchment and add the two rolled-out breads to the pan. Fry for 2–3 minutes, turning once, until brown patches have appeared.

4 Remove from the pan and keep warm in a clean dish towel. Continue rolling and cooking the flatbreads in batches until they are all cooked. Serve while still warm with hummus.

HEALTH NOTE Coeliac disease is often misunderstood and thought by many to be a food allergy or food intolerance but it is actually an auto-immune disease. The body reacts to gluten, found mostly in wheat and some grains, as if it were a foreign substance, so that vital nutrients are not absorbed by the body. Keep a separate set of chopping boards, bowls etc for gluten-free cooking so that there is no chance of cross-contamination with wheat-based foods.

MAKES 12

Prep 30 minutes
Rest 15 minutes
Cook 15 minutes

200g/7oz/2 cups gram or chickpea flour, sifted

150g/5oz/1 cup rice flour

2.5ml/½ tsp salt

2.5ml/½ tsp xanthum gum, optional

15ml/1 tbsp za'atar spice mix, see page 29

25g/1oz butter, melted

250–300ml/8–10fl oz/ 1–1¼ cup cold water

30–45ml/2–3 tbsp sunflower oil

Cinnamon apple and hummus muffins

MAKES 12

Prep 15 minutes
Cook 20 minutes

110g/4oz/½ cup hummus,
see page 36 or hummus
of choice without garlic

3 eggs

120ml/4fl oz/½ cup milk

5ml/1 tsp vanilla extract

1 x 175g/6oz dessert apple,
cored but not peeled,
coarsely grated

1 small banana, 125g/4½oz
in its skin, peeled and
mashed with a fork

150g/5oz/1 cup rice flour

5ml/1 tsp gluten-free baking
powder

5ml/1 tsp ground cinnamon

75g/3oz/½ cup light
muscovado (brown) or caster
(superfine) sugar

30ml/2 tbsp sunflower or
pumpkin seeds, optional

This bake isn't just to eat with hummus, but has hummus in it! Hummus adds a high-protein boost to this easy-to-mix lunchbox treat and means that you don't need to add extra butter or oil. Mixed with rice flour, these muffins are gluten-free and if you swap the milk for your favourite nut milk they can be dairy-free too.

1 Preheat the oven to 190°C/375°F/Gas 5. Line a 12-hole muffin tin or pan with squares of baking parchment or small paper cases, or lightly brush the tin sections with a little oil.

2 Add the hummus, eggs, milk and vanilla to a bowl and fork together to mix, then stir in the apple and banana. In a second larger bowl add the rice flour, baking powder, cinnamon and sugar and stir together. Add the wet ingredients to the dry, fork together until just mixed then pour into the sections of the oiled muffin tin.

3 Sprinkle the tops with the seeds and bake for about 20 minutes until well risen and slightly cracked on top. Leave to cool for 5 minutes then loosen the muffins with a knife, turn out and cool on a wire rack. Best served within 24 hours of making.

Energy 132kcal/553kJ; Protein 3.9g; Carbohydrate 22.2g, of which sugars 11.1g; Fat 3.1g, of which saturates 0.7g; Cholesterol 58mg; Calcium 29mg; Fibre 1.1g; Sodium 89mg.

Index